The Prado Museum Expansion

REACTING TO THE PAST is an award-winning series of immersive role-playing games that actively engage students in their own learning. Students assume the roles of historical characters and practice critical thinking, primary source analysis, and argument, both written and spoken. Reacting games are flexible enough to be used across the curriculum, from first-year general education classes and discussion sections of lecture classes to capstone experiences, intersession courses, and honors programs.

Reacting to the Past was originally developed under the auspices of Barnard College and is sustained by the Reacting Consortium of colleges and universities. The Consortium hosts a regular series of conferences and events to support faculty and administrators.

NOTE TO INSTRUCTORS: Before beginning the game you must download the game materials, including an instructor's manual containing a detailed schedule of class sessions, role sheets for students, and handouts.

To download these essential resources, visit https://reactingconsortium.org/games, click on the page for this title, then click "Game Materials."

The Prado Museum Expansion

THE DIVERSE ART
OF LATIN AMERICA

BRIDGET V. FRANCO

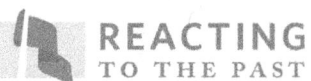

BARNARD

The University of North Carolina Press

Chapel Hill

Cover art: Joaquín Torres García (1878–49),
América Invertida, 1943. Courtesy Wikimedia Commons.

ISBN 978-1-4696-7685-2 (pbk.: alk. paper)

ISBN 978-1-4696-7686-9 (e-book)

Excerpt from *Manifestos and Polemics in Latin American Modern Art*, edited and translated by Patrick Frank, copyright © 2017 University of New Mexico Press

Contents

Illustrations

The Prado
Museum
Expansion

1

Introduction

From 2001 to 2007, the world-renowned Prado Museum in Madrid, Spain, underwent an ambitious expansion project that reorganized the museum's spatial design and significantly increased the available exhibition space. Coinciding with the completion of this large construction project was a series of celebrations surrounding the 2010 bicentenary of South American independence movements, a clear reminder of the complicated relationship between Spain and its former colonies in Latin America. Inspired by this significant historical moment and with an eye to diversifying its predominantly Spanish-centered permanent collection, the Prado Museum decides to host a competition for a new gallery of Latin American art.

The game opens in 2010 as the curators set into motion a series of negotiation sessions to help them decide which artworks to choose for the new gallery. The curators must think carefully about how best to craft their joint vision for this gallery. Which paintings are essential to understand contemporary Latin American art? How will they create a coherent vision for the new museum space? Who is the public for this new exhibit? What will they expect to see? What geographical, historical, political, and artistic factors must the curators take into account when selecting their pieces?

The Prado Museum administration has already made a preliminary selection of paintings from Argentina, Brazil, Chile, Colombia, Costa Rica, Cuba, Ecuador, Mexico, Peru, Puerto Rico, and Uruguay. The artists and the art dealers who hold the rights to these paintings have all flown to Madrid and are staying at the nearby hotel Catalonia Las Cortes. The Prado has also invited an important patron of the arts and a private collector to participate in the selection process as a means of securing financial support for the new gallery. The meetings will take place in the museum itself.

The art dealers' and living artists' main objective is to successfully secure a place for their painting in the new gallery at the Prado. To achieve this goal, they

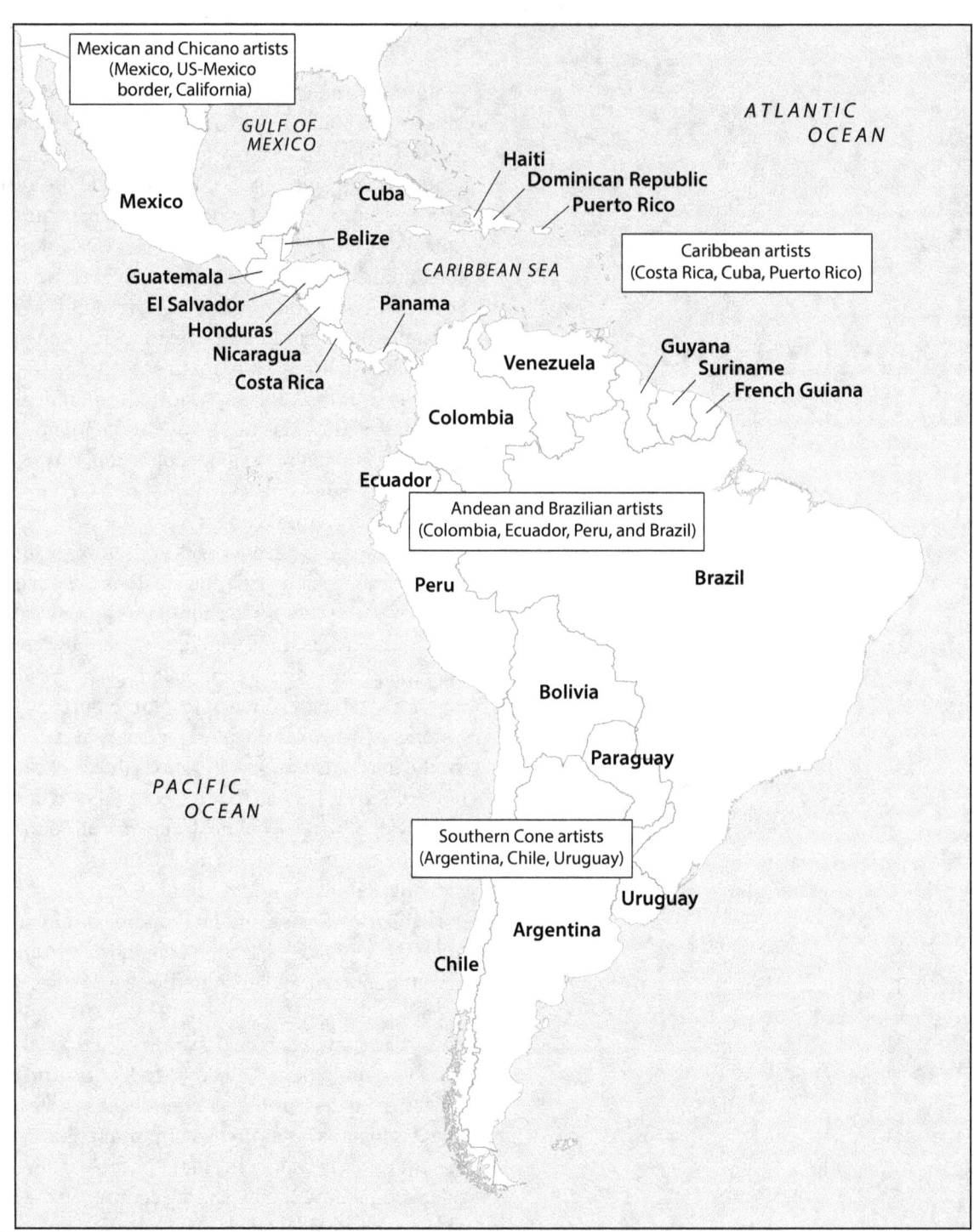

Latin America showing geographic factions

will need to be prepared to explain the importance of their paintings to the curators, the patron of the arts, and the private collector. They may also need to negotiate with other players to ensure a favorable outcome. For the living artists who are less well-known than their deceased compatriots, there is a particular sense of urgency, as they must claim their rightful place in the vast world of Latin American art. For the art dealers, securing a place for their artist's painting at the prestigious Prado Museum would be an enormous professional accomplishment. At the same time, the art dealers must always have their eyes open for new, up-and-coming artists who may be in search of expert representation.

The patron of the arts and the private collector are both art lovers, each in their own way. Their tastes are specific and grounded in works of art that they are already familiar with. They are also open-minded about expanding their collections, however, and are very interested in hearing from the art dealers and artists about why their particular painting is unique and important. Given their sizable wealth and access to resources in the art world, the patron and the private collector should be treated with the utmost respect and attention by all players.

The Prado Museum Expansion offers a chance to view, analyze, and debate a range of artistic movements and styles related to Latin American art from the twentieth century through the early twenty-first. Players will have an opportunity to discuss many questions: for example, What does diversity in art mean? What are some distinguishing characteristics of contemporary Latin American artistic movements? What are the salient characteristics of Latin American painting? In what ways do Latin American artists dialogue with European artists? What are some of the historical power issues at play between Spain and Latin America? How does art interface with history?

Playing the Game in Spanish

The *Prado* game was originally designed to be played in Spanish-language courses at the intermediate or advanced level. Since then, the game has been adapted so that it can be played in either English and Spanish for courses in writing and conversation, Latin American culture, Spanish and Latin American art history, and women in Latin America. The instructions in the game book are provided in English for clarity, convenience, and pedagogical ease, but you also will find materials to facilitate game play in Spanish, such as translations of key vocabulary lists, artistic movements/styles, and other relevant information. The game manager (GM) may also distribute additional resources to support game play *en español*.

Guide to Spanish Vocabulary

See table 1 for a list of frequently used Spanish terms in the game book and their English translations. See also the appendix, which contains an expanded Spanish/English glossary with useful terms for talking and writing about art.

TABLE 1 Frequently used non-English terms in the game book

Term (Spanish unless otherwise noted)	English translation or definition
abaporu	cannibal (from Indigenous language Tupí Guaraní)
antropofagia	cannibalism, anthropophagy (from Portuguese)
barrio	neighborhood
carteles	road signs
catador	garbage pickers of recyclable materials (from Portuguese)
Círculo y Cuadrado	Circle and Square (from French, Cercle et Carré)
compadre	compatriot, buddy, pal
compañero	comrade, companion, teammate
docente	museum docent, guide
Duque	duke
el coloso	colossus, giant
escrache	acts of public shaming
feria	street fair
madrileño	person from Madrid, Spain
maestro	master, teacher
Museo de Bellas Artes	Museum of Fine Arts
neocriollo	Neo-Creole, the name of an invented language derived from Spanish and Portuguese, with bits of French, English, and Guaraní
norteño	person from the northern region of Mexico
obras de arte	works of art
los tres grandes	the three great ones: that is, the Mexican muralists Diego Rivera, José Clemente Orozco, and David Alfaro Siqueiros

PROLOGUE

In the following vignette, imagine that you are a contemporary Latin American artist on your way to the Prado Museum in Madrid. This is an opportunity for you to convince the renowned museum that your work should be displayed in the new exhibit on modern Latin American art.

Sitting in an airplane, you reflect on the unique opportunity before you. You are on your way to the Prado Museum in Spain for one of the most important gatherings of your career. The curators of the Prado have decided to install an exhibit on Latin American art, and they have selected you and other Latin American artists to come share your work with a wider audience. You are on your way to convince the curators that your piece is worthy of the Prado—and you know this will not be an easy task. You know that the other artists too are talented and passionate, and this would be an incredible honor for any of you.

You look out the window and see white clouds against the backdrop of a clear blue sky. The beauty is breathtaking, yet you cannot fully appreciate this majesty because the nerves in your stomach are distracting your mind. Sipping on water, you think about the piece of art you have brought with you. You wonder if you made the right choice, but you know there is no turning back now. You have put everything into your art. You have dedicated countless hours to perfecting it. You know your work deserves to be in the Prado, but you have to convince the curators of this. Since not every piece of art will be accepted for the new exhibit, you must to do everything you can to ensure that your piece is selected.

You close your eyes, hoping to rest before the long days ahead of you. But your mind is racing, considering all the things you could possibly say to defend your piece. You are aware that a wide range of art will be represented and that the curators are looking for the artworks that best represent Latin America.

As a Latin American artist, you know that your art represents your culture, but you also know that Latin America is an extremely diverse region, both culturally and geographically. There is no single defining characteristic that represents all of Latin America, so you wonder how the curators are going to determine which pieces to exhibit. You must form your own opinion on what Latin American art is so that you can convince the curators, the patron of the arts, and the private collector that your vision is the best one for the Prado. You have your own perspective of Latin American culture that you want to share with the world, but you should also listen to the ideas of other artists and art dealers and understand each unique perspective.

Art can reflect important topics and difficult issues. You imagine that some of the artists will speak about gender, some about race, some about politics, and some about culture. There will be significant questions raised in the sessions at the Prado. What roles do marginalized voices play in Latin American culture and art? What perspectives can women add to historical narratives dominated by male artists? How are different racial and ethnic identities expressed through art? Should art intentionally address issues of race, gender, religion, and politics, or should paintings be valued purely for aesthetic reasons? You have already begun thinking about these questions. Ultimately, you must decide how your art relates to these themes and what messages you would like to send.

The changing shapes of the clouds in the sky outside your plane window remind you of the different artistic styles and movements that have found a place in twentieth-century Latin American art. There will no doubt be paintings that represent expressionism, a movement whose distorted, colorful images provoke strong emotional reactions. You will probably also see pieces with the childlike simplicity of naïve art and the sharp photographic qualities of hyperrealism. There will be cubist paintings, highly geometric art, and, similarly, constructivist pieces with strong lines and heavily defined forms. You expect to find wonderfully dreamlike surrealist paintings, and of course the large-scale Mexican murals, with their realistic portrayal of urban life in the 1920s and 1930s. You have also heard rumors about new kinds of art such as Verdadism and street art, both of which call the viewer to action through social commentary and political provocation. Among these different styles, you will find different techniques and diverse mediums. By participating in this competition, you also hope to find inspiration for future creations.

Thinking about this vast diversity of art is exciting—you will be able to view art that is so different from your own but created by equally passionate artists. You will hear different perspectives from many talented individuals. This will be an incredible opportunity to share your art, to learn from the other artists, and to meet people who could promote your work—and, of course, a once-in-a-lifetime chance to have your painting included in the renowned Prado Museum.

You hear the voice of the pilot announcing that the plane will be landing soon at Barajas International Airport in Madrid, Spain. You are almost there. It is almost time for you to meet the curators and the other artists. This is not the time for nerves, you tell yourself. This is the time for you to boldly speak for your art, to advocate for your experience, and to share with the Prado, and hopefully the world, that your art is a true representation of Latin American art and culture. *¡Vámonos!*

BASIC FEATURES OF REACTING TO THE PAST

This is a historical role-playing game set in a moment of heightened historical tension; it places you in the role of a person from the period. After a few preparatory lectures, the game begins and the students are in charge. By reading the game book and your individual role sheet, you will find out more about your objectives, worldview, allies, and opponents. You must then attempt to achieve victory through formal speeches, informal debate, negotiations, and conspiracy. Outcomes sometimes differ from actual history; a debriefing session sets the record straight. What follows is an outline of what you will encounter in Reacting and what you will be expected to do.

Game Setup

Your instructor will spend some time before the beginning of the game helping you to understand the historical context for the game. During the setup period, you will use several different kinds of material:

- The game book (what you are reading now), which includes historical information, rules and elements of the game, and essential historical documents.
- A role sheet, which provides a short biography of the historical person you will model in the game as well as that person's ideology, objectives, responsibilities, and resources. Some roles are based on historical figures. Others are "composites," with elements drawn from a number of individuals. You will receive your role sheet from your instructor.

Familiarize yourself with the documents before the game begins and return to them once you are in role. They contain information and arguments that will be useful as the game unfolds. A second reading while in role will deepen your understanding and alter your perspective. Once the game is in motion, your perspectives may change. Some ideas may begin to look quite different. Those who have carefully read the materials and who know the rules of the game will invariably do better than those who rely on general impressions and uncertain memories.

Game Play

Once the game begins, class sessions are run by students. In most cases, a single student serves as a sort of presiding officer. The instructor then becomes the GM (the "game master" or "game manager") and takes a seat in the back of the room. Though they do not lead the class sessions, GMs may do any of the following:

- Pass notes
- Announce important events
- Redirect proceedings that have gone off track

Instructors are, of course, available for consultations before and after game sessions. Although they will not let you in on any of the secrets of the game, they can be invaluable in terms of sharpening your arguments or finding key historical resources.

The presiding officer is expected to observe basic standards of fairness, but as a fail-safe device, most games employ the "podium rule," which allows a student who has not been recognized to approach the podium and wait for a chance to speak. Once at the podium, the student has the floor and must be heard.

Role sheets contain private, secret information that you must guard. Exercise caution when discussing your role with others. Your role sheet probably identifies likely allies, but even they may not always be trustworthy. However, keeping your own counsel and saying nothing to anyone is not an option. To achieve your objectives, you must speak with others. You will never muster the voting strength to prevail without allies. Collaboration and coalition building are at the heart of every game.

Some games feature strong alliances called factions. As a counterbalance, these games include roles called indeterminates. They operate outside the established factions, and while some are entirely neutral, most possess their own idiosyncratic objectives. If you are in a faction, cultivating indeterminates is in your interest, since they can be persuaded to support your position. If you are lucky enough to have drawn the role of an indeterminate, you should be pleased: you will likely play a pivotal role in the outcome of the game.

Game Requirements

Students playing Reacting games practice persuasive writing, public speaking, critical thinking, teamwork, negotiation, problem solving, collaboration, adapting to changing circumstances, and working under pressure to meet deadlines. Your instructor will explain the specific requirements for your class. In general, though, a Reacting game asks you to perform three distinct activities:

Reading and writing. What you read can often be put to immediate use, and what you write is meant to persuade others to act the way you want them to. The reading load may vary slightly from role to role; the writing requirement depends on your particular course. Papers are often policy statements, but they can also be autobiographies, battle plans, newspaper articles, poems, or after-game reflections. Papers often provide the foundation for the speeches delivered in class. They also help to familiarize you with the issues, which should allow you to ask good questions.

Public speaking and debate. In the course of a game, almost everyone is expected to deliver at least one formal speech from the podium (the length of the game and the size of the class will determine the number of speeches). Debate follows. It can be impromptu, raucous, and fast paced. At some point, discussions must lead to action, which often means proposing, debating, and passing a variety of resolutions. GMs may stipulate that students must deliver their papers from memory when at the podium, or they may insist that students begin to wean themselves from dependency on written notes as the game progresses.

Wherever the game imaginatively puts you, it will surely not put you in the present. Accordingly, the colloquialisms and familiarities of today's college life are out of place. Never open your speech with a salutation like "Hi guys" when something like "Fellow citizens!" would be more appropriate.

Always seek allies to back your points when you are speaking at the podium. Do your best to have at least one supporter second your proposal, come to your defense, or admonish inattentive members of the body. Note-passing and side conversations, while common occurrences, will likely spoil the effect of your speech, so you and your supporters should insist on order before such behavior becomes too disruptive. Ask the presiding officer to assist you. Appeal to the GM as a last resort.

Strategizing. Communication among students is an essential feature of Reacting games. You will likely find yourself writing emails, texting, attending out-of-class meetings, or gathering for meals. The purpose of frequent communication is to lay out a strategy for achieving your objectives, thwarting your opponents, and hatching plots. When communicating with fellow students in or out of class, always assume that they are speaking to you in role. If you want to talk about the "real world," make that clear.

CONTROVERSY

Most Reacting games take place at moments of conflict in the past and therefore are likely to address difficult, even painful, issues that we continue to grapple with today. Consequently, this game may contain controversial subject matter. You may need to represent ideas with which you personally disagree or that you even find repugnant. When speaking about these ideas, make it clear that you are speaking in role. Furthermore, if other people say things that offend you, recognize that they too are playing roles. If you decide to respond to them, do so using the voice of your role and make this clear. If these efforts are insufficient, or the ideas associated with your particular role seem potentially overwhelming, talk to your GM.

When playing your role, rely on your role sheet and the other game materials rather than drawing on caricature or stereotype. Do not use racial and ethnic slurs even if they are historically appropriate. If you are concerned about the potential for cultural appropriation or the use of demeaning language in your game, talk to your GM.

Amid the plotting, debating, and voting, always remember that this is an immersive role-playing game. Other players may resist your efforts, attack your ideas, and even betray a confidence. They take these actions because they are playing their roles. If you become concerned about the potential for game-based conflict to bleed out into the real world, take a step back and reflect on the situation. If your concerns persist, talk to your GM.

COUNTERFACTUALS

The Prado Museum's expansion project (2001–7) did indeed occur, resulting in a new visitor center (in Rafael Moneo's cube-shaped building located near the Jerónimo cloisters) and exhibition display space for an additional 400–500 works. And while the Prado Museum was involved in the 2010 traveling exhibition *Painting from the Viceroyalties* to mark the bicentenary of the independence movements in South America, the institution did not diversify their permanent collection to create a new gallery of contemporary Latin American painting in 2010. The director and museum administration instead remained committed to museum's traditional identity as an institution of Spanish national art from the twelfth to twentieth centuries. The rival Reina Sofia Museum in Madrid, however, did organize a temporary exhibition on Latin American art in 2000–2001, which included works by Frida Kahlo, Joaquín Torres García, David Alfaro Siqueiros, Tarsila do Amaral, and Vik Muniz. During the final debriefing session, the GM will provide information about the Prado Museum's more recent efforts to diversify its exhibitions.

2

Historical Background

THE ART WORLD

Prado Museum Expansion

Beginning in 2002, then–Prado Museum director Miguel Zugaza oversaw an ambitious plan known as the *expansión*, a multiyear project that would rearrange and expand the permanent display of art in the world-renowned Spanish museum. The plan resulted in a significant increase in display space that was recuperated following the relocation of the restoration workshops, gift shop, temporary galleries, café/restaurant, and tourist information centers to a new cube-shaped building designed by Rafael Moneo. The newly available space meant that an additional 400–500 artworks could be shown, in addition to the thousands of pieces (paintings, drawings, prints, and sculptures) already in the permanent display. Most of these additional pieces came from the Prado's own holdings, which comprise the world's largest collection of Spanish national artworks, spanning from the twelfth century to the twentieth. Indeed, the core of the museum's collection comes from royal holdings, including pieces by court painters like Diego de Velázquez and Francisco de Goya, as well as a variety of medieval and Renaissance paintings. In addition to the museum's strong national focus, there are some acquisitions from other parts of the world, including Latin America. Many of the art pieces from Latin America, such as Talavera ceramics, Alcora pottery, and other pre-Columbian artifacts, were acquired by the museum through the Pedro Fernández Durán Bequest of 1930. But when the expansion project was completed in 2007, the Prado Museum did not have a permanent gallery of Latin American art.

Coinciding with the completion of the museum's large construction project was a series of celebrations surrounding the 2010 bicentenary of South American independence movements, a clear reminder of the complicated relationship between Spain and its former colonies in Latin America. In 2010, to mark the bicentenary of the independence movements in South America, a group of interested parties including Fomento Cultural Banamex, Patrimonio

Nacional, and the Prado Museum collaborated on a traveling exhibition titled *Painting from the Viceroyalties*. Featuring more than 100 works, it offered a visual reflection of the cultural relationship between Europe, particularly Spain, and the South American viceroyalties in the sixteenth through eighteenth centuries. The Prado Museum was energized by the enthusiastic response to this collaborative exhibition and excited about pursuing other opportunities to diversify their collections and update their traditional and, for some art critics, antiquated reputation.

Museum Dynamics and Exhibition Curation

In our game, inspired by this successful international initiative, the Prado Museum administration decides to take advantage of the new spaces created during the expansion to diversify their permanent collection and create a gallery of Latin American painting as part of a broadening focus on the diverse art of Latin America. Two Prado Museum curators, played by composite characters Nuria Hernández and Roberto Pérez, have been tasked with deciding which works will be hung in the new gallery. The curators have different but complementary areas of expertise that will ensure a balanced mix of artworks from the twentieth and twenty-first centuries. The Prado Museum administration has invited a patron of the arts, el Duque de Artega (the Duke of Artega), to participate in the selection process, in gratitude for his generous past donations. The curators have also asked el señor Lustres, a private collector of contemporary art, to attend the sessions and lend his expertise to the process of creating a diverse selection of gallery paintings.

The game opens in 2010 as the curators set into motion a series of negotiation sessions that will help them decide, in collaboration with the Duque de Artega and Sr. Lustres, which artworks to choose for the new gallery. The curators must think carefully about how best to craft their joint vision for this gallery. Which Latin American paintings are essential to enable an understanding of contemporary Latin

American art? How will they create a coherent vision for the new museum space? Who is the public for this new exhibit? What will they expect to see? What geographical, historical, political, and artistic factors must they take into account when choosing their pieces?

During the selection process, the curators of the gallery must wrestle with important questions about how to frame and define the exhibit. Are issues of geographic diversity important? What are the geopolitical boundaries of Latin American art? Should works from non-Spanish-speaking countries be included? Can Latin American or Latino/a artists living in the United States be considered? Which artistic styles and movements are most important to recognize and display? Are there styles that are unique to Latin America, or should there be an emphasis on works with influences from European art? Is the political and historical context of the works significant? Should the exhibit frame the paintings through an ideological lens or focus on "art for art's sake"? What role do issues of gender and race play?

Twentieth-Century Latin American Art

Twentieth-century Latin American art spans a richly diverse panorama of artists from roughly twenty different countries. The curators have selected pieces from artists hailing from Argentina, Brazil, Chile, Colombia, Costa Rica, Cuba, Ecuador, Uruguay, Mexico, Peru, and Puerto Rico in an attempt to highlight the region's geographic breadth. Half of the paintings are by deceased artists who are represented at the competition by their respective art dealers. These well-known paintings masterfully demonstrate the influence of cubism, surrealism, constructivism, expressionism, *indigenismo*, and muralism in modern Latin American art. Many of these artistic styles are grounded in the European avant-garde movements of the first half of the twentieth century, clearly connecting artistic innovations from Spain, France, and Italy to the development of modern Latin American art. While many Latin American artists traveled to Europe in their early years, they would not claim to have simply imitated their European counterparts.

In fact, some artists, like Joaquín Torres García, were instrumental in contributing to the development of certain avant-garde styles, such as constructivism, during their travels in Europe. Other artists, like the Cuban painter Wifredo Lam, fused the formal elements of surrealism with the reality of his Afro-Caribbean experience to represent the colonial legacy of exploitation and slavery in Latin America. Tarsila do Amaral referred to her desire to devour and suppress European art styles in her work and incorporate Indigenous cultural references in order to produce uniquely Brazilian art. Indeed, one of the central tensions in the negotiations will be between the undeniable influence of European artistic movements, especially in terms of formal technique, and the artists' need to identify as Latin American or, more specifically, Brazilian, Cuban, or Mexican.

Additionally, the curators have invited a variety of young artists to the competition. While these artists are competing against important artworks that represent an array of well-known artistic movements from the first half of the twentieth century, they are also excited to show how they are forging new paths for Latin American art as we move into the twenty-first century. These new artists will push the boundaries established by their predecessors. Many of them are uninterested in the elitist idea of "art for art's sake" and are more concerned with creating and displaying art in different formats for people of all ages, from all walks of life. Does where you come from have to define what kind of art you make? These young artists are proud of their heritage and culture, but they do not believe that geographic or national boundaries should define art from or about Latin America. More importantly, many of these young artists see inequities in their daily lives, and they want their artwork to encourage people to think about the power dynamics related to questions of race, gender, economics, politics, and religion.

Finally, the Latin American artists and art dealers will have the unique opportunity to network and get to know one another, in the hopes of establishing a connection that will result in a professional relationship that will last beyond the Prado competition.

The lesser-known artists from Latin America must think about the trajectory of their career, and they are looking to sign a contract with one of the art dealers to ensure that their future work is protected and promoted. However, it is in everyone's best interest to connect artists with art dealers whose expertise and aesthetic are compatible.

ARTISTIC MOVEMENTS AND STYLES

The following summary contributed by Lisa Crossman, curator of American Art and Arts of the Americas at the Mead Art Museum (Amherst College), illustrates the vast array of artistic movements and styles related to Latin American art in the twentieth and twenty-first centuries. See table 2 for a chronology of artistic movements and their characteristics.

Avant-Garde (*La vanguardia*)

Avant-garde (literally "advance guard" or "vanguard" in English) originated as a French term that referred to the group of troops that forged ahead of the rest of the army. It was adopted as a cultural reference in nineteenth-century France, first used in relation to the visual arts in the 1850s to place realism as a vanguard movement. The term then came to encompass other innovative and experimental modern art movements, such as surrealism, cubism, and futurism. Each, in its own way, pushed the boundaries of art making. Movements like cubism were preoccupied with formal issues. Others, including surrealism, used new techniques to respond to social concerns and advancements.

Numerous Latin American artists traveled to major art centers in Europe like Paris to study in the late nineteenth and early twentieth centuries. With this training, some artists synthesized aspects of movements such as cubism and futurism, developing innovative practices that continued to mature after those artists returned to their native countries in the 1920s. Argentina, Mexico, and Brazil in particular were home to a florescence of avant-garde production in this decade. The anthropophagy embodied by Tarsila do Amaral's paintings in Brazil, the Florida (focused on formal experimentation) and Boedo (socially minded and leftist leaning) groups in Argentina, and muralism in Mexico were innovative movements that departed from European models and thus mark the development of an avant-garde in these nations. It is notable that some avant-gardes, such as Mexican muralism, explicitly focused on national identity, whereas others, like those in Buenos Aires,

were more concerned with aesthetics and the cosmopolitan. Writers and visual artists were also strongly linked. For instance, Tarsila do Amaral's painting *Abaporu* (a Tupi Guarani word that means "man who eats man") came to epitomize the principal tenets of Oswald de Andrade's "Manifesto Antropófago" ("Cannibalist Manifesto") of 1928. It proposes cannibalism as a symbolic means of consuming European models and transforming them into new Latin American art forms.

As liberal governments were overtaken by more conservative ones in the 1930s in nations like Argentina and Brazil, avant-garde production was momentarily sidelined. Avant-gardes in other parts of Latin America, including the Andean nations, emerged a bit later, in the 1930s and 1940s, with an *indigenista* (nativist) movement.

Cubism (*El cubismo*)

Cubism was one of the most influential innovations in art of the twentieth century. As rapid industrialization took place in city centers, along with the advent of fast-moving modes of transport, visual artists sought to capture this new way of experiencing their world. Cubists focused on formal concerns, depicting multiple angles of an object to give the suggestion of movement and the passage of time. George Braque (1882–1963) and Pablo Picasso (1881–1973) collaborated on the various stages of cubism's development. Cubist paintings broke everyday objects into distinct planes and reorganized them on the canvas to show forms from different perspectives, resulting in a distorted, geometric image. Picasso's celebrated painting *Las Señoritas de Avignon* (1907) reflects his comment "I paint objects as I think them, not as I see them."

The first phase is called analytic cubism, involving a systematic study and close observation of objects in monochromatic tones. The subject matter was restricted to still life and portraiture. Synthetic cubism grew from the first when these artists began to incorporate collage. The introduction of other media completely broke away from traditional rendering of space and a more conceptual depiction

TABLE 2 Chronology of artistic movements

Period	Movement	Characteristics
1907–14	Cubism	Rejection of the idea that art should copy reality or nature. Rejection of traditional techniques of perspective and modeling. Attention to the two-dimensionality of the canvas; reduction of the objects into geometric forms, multiple vantage points.
1905–25	Expressionism	Image of reality is distorted to express the artist's inner feelings. Color can be highly intense and nonnaturalistic.
1915–34	Constructivism, constructive universalism	Borrowed ideas from cubism; sought to abolish the traditional artistic concern with composition and replace it with construction. Objects were to be created not to express beauty or the artist's outlook, or to represent the world, but to carry out a fundamental analysis of the materials and forms of art.
1920–39	Surrealism	Exploration of the unconscious through art; dreamlike landscapes, erotically explicit objects. Surprising imagery, deep symbolism, refined painting techniques, disdain for convention.
1920–30	Mexican muralism	Large-scale mural painting designed to convey social and political messages to the masses.
1930–40	Indigenismo	Subjects represented are Indigenous people of Latin America; can depict national pride of ancient heritage or refer to marginalization of contemporary Indigenous and mestizo members of society.
1940–50	Abstract expressionism	Monumentally scaled works that reflect the artist's psyche, with an emphasis on spontaneity, improvisation, and process, using gestural brushstrokes and primarily abstract imagery. Verdadism (1990s) is a more recent style of abstract expressionism.
1960s–70s	Chicano/a art	Part of the political and cultural movement to defend the civil rights of working-class Mexicans and Mexican Americans in California. The artwork challenged different aspects of mainstream representation of Mexican American identities.
1960s–present day	Street art	Created in public locations, usually unsanctioned, using common materials; collective, reflecting a diversity of expressions (performance, happenings, installations, videos, interventions).
1990s–2000s	Hyperrealism	Highly precise re-creations of photographic images through painting; the earlier photorealist movement arose in the 1960s–70s in response to the nonfigurative, subjective focus of abstract expressionism. Twenty-first-century hyperrealism borrows the realistic techniques of photorealism but plays with the images for political or social purposes.
Twentieth century (throughout)	Naïve, or naïf, art	Childlike simplicity of execution and vision. Typically has a flat rendering style with a rudimentary expression of perspective. Strong use of pattern or color without differentiating between foreground and background.

of objects emerged. In this later phase, Picasso also experimented with sculptural assemblage.

Cubism became a point of reference for many Latin American avant-gardes of the twentieth century. Diego Rivera studied in Europe, and by 1913 he produced cubist paintings with references to his Mexican culture. This formative period would later inform Rivera's dynamic compositions in mural painting. The Argentine Emilio Pettoruti (1892–1971) is one artist who effectively fused cubism and futurism. Pettoruti produced a series of still lifes, as well as interior and street views. One prominent work that focuses on tango musicians, *The Quintet*, recalls Picasso's *Three Musicians*. Pettoruti composed his fragmented figures in a cubist style, but he applied bright colors in varying tonalities in an effort to depict light's radiance, which fascinated the futurists. Both Rivera and Pettoruti are examples of Latin American artists experimenting with degrees of abstraction, distilling elements from European models to achieve their own visual language.

Expressionism (*El expresionismo*)

Expressionism is an international movement in art and architecture that flourished in the first few decades of the twentieth century, particularly in Germany. Expressionist painting was a response against academic training and impressionism, seeking to move away from empirical observations toward more humanistic interests. In an effort to communicate the spiritual condition, these artists made use of symbolic and heightened color, assertive forms, and aggressive brushwork. Ernst Ludwig Kirchner (1880–1938) was an important German expressionist whose canvases portrayed the anxieties of urban society and the tensions leading up to World War I. He rendered highly stylized figures with swift angular forms and nervous hatching to emphasize the feeling of unease that defined the urban experience.

"Expressionism" is also used interchangeably with "postimpressionism," and although it was established in the early twentieth century, it has since been foundational for later movements. Abstract expressionism in the United States and Art Informel in France, as well as neoexpressionism from the 1980s, are all indebted to early modern expressionism. In Latin America, neofiguration artists were informed by these earlier interests in the symbolic use of color and the psychological tensions suggested in form and texture. These formal solutions were primarily sought to address social concerns. José Luis Cuevas (1934–2017) was a catalyst in Mexico. He challenged the institutionalization and political art of the Mexican muralists and introduced an expressionist distortion of the figure with a focus on the individual psyche. Venezuelan artist Jacobo Borges (b. 1931) was more political than most of his neofiguration contemporaries, as a result of Venezuela's ten-year dictatorship in the 1950s. Working on large-scale canvases, Borges applied rigorous line and bold color to portray half-blurred images, suggesting flashbacks and vague memories of a suppressive regime. Neofiguration artists took advantage of the expressive qualities in paint application to portray the contemporary condition of their urbanizing societies.

Constructivism and Constructive Universalism (*El constructivismo y el universalismo constructivo*)

Among the avant-garde movements that developed across Latin America in the 1930s through 1950s were artists who created new forms of geometric abstraction. These movements had a basis in European models such as constructivism, concrete art, and neoplasticism. In Russia around 1915, Vladimir Tatlin and Alexander Rodchenko established constructivism—a new aesthetic that would reflect the industrial, modern world. Like many avant-garde movements, constructivism responded to national and sociopolitical changes. Its ideas, initially inspired by cubism, stimulated other artists in Russia and beyond.

The constructive universalism of Uruguayan artist Joaquín Torres García (1874–1949) had an impact on artists throughout the region, as it represented a mode of geometric abstraction rooted in Latin America and an inversion of Eurocentric cultural hierarchies. Torres García, having participated in European avant-garde movements during his forty-three years abroad, returned to Uruguay in 1934. Notably, before leaving Europe he founded Cercle et Carré (Circle and Square)—an association that fostered abstraction—with Piet Mondrian and Michel Seuphor in 1929. In Montevideo, Uruguay, Torres García continued his unique advancement of abstraction through the development of constructive universalism. It drew from cubism, neoplasticism, and constructivism, but also integrated ideas and symbols inspired by pre-Columbian art and local vernacular imagery. The use of a grid pattern most succinctly embodied constructivist traditions. Torres García was not interested in creating an art that reflected industry, however; instead he used the grid to order the pictographs that populated his compositions. The pictographs were universal, and the paintings always looked handmade. In addition, constructivist pieces are known for the importance of technique and process in the elaboration of the artwork, the predominance of three-dimensionality, the rejection of decorative accents, the use of simple materials (wood, metal, wire, plaster, plastic, cardboard), and certain colors, including orange, red, yellow, black, and white.

Torres García founded the Asociación de Arte Constructivo (Association of Constructive Art, 1935–39) and the Taller Torres García (Torres García Workshop, 1943–62) through which he disseminated his ideas. He also published *Círculo y Cuadrado*, his own Spanish-language version of *Cercle et Carré*, and the widely cited manifesto *La Escuela del Sur* (School of the South), which inspired new thinking around geometric abstraction and Eurocentric art hierarchies. Constructive universalism was a regional movement that legitimized the South as an area with its own rich cultural traditions.

Other artists developed new models of concrete art (a term that refers to abstraction that is not representational in any way and is free of symbolic association). Taking Swiss artist Max Bill as a model, groups like Arte Concreto Invención, Asociación Arte Concreto-Invención, y Grupo Madí in Argentina, and Grupo Ruptura and Grupo Frente in Brazil,

experimented with nonobjective art in the 1940s and 1950s.

Surrealism (*El surrealismo*)

Surrealism developed in the 1910s and 1920s as a literary movement and soon came to include visual artists. Following on the heels of Dada, surrealism rejected the rational in favor of automatism, dreams, the uncanny, and free association. André Breton, a poet, critic, and trained psychologist, published the *Surrealist Manifesto* in Paris in 1924. He drew on Sigmund Freud's psychological theories, including Freud's work on the unconscious mind and dreams, and Karl Marx's political theories. There are two broad types of surrealism: the oneiric (dreamlike imagery) and automatism (a creative process that unleashed the unconscious by drawing or writing without conscious thought).

After the onset of World War II, the surrealists disbanded as a cohesive group. Breton visited Mexico in 1938 and organized an exhibition of surrealist art there in 1940, which included work by artists such as Frida Kahlo (1907–54). While Latin American artists were exposed to surrealism in Europe and adapted certain aspects of it, there was not a cohesive surrealist movement in the region. Still, some artists who were from Latin American nations or who moved to the region were surrealists. For instance, Roberto Matta (Chile, 1911–2002) was part of the European movement, and Wifredo Lam (Cuba, 1902–82) identified as such. Others, including Leonora Carrington (England, 1917–2011) and Remedios Varo (Spain, 1908–63), both produced surrealist works while living in Mexico. In Latin America, artists seemed more apt to gravitate toward its potential to explore identity and psychological independence than to center on automatic techniques.

Mexican Muralism (*El muralismo mexicano*)

Mexican muralism developed in the wake of the Mexican Revolution (1910–20) as part of state-sponsored nation building. Mexican muralism, unlike most avant-gardes, received government funding to support the creation of large-scale, public murals, beginning under the presidency of Álvaro Obregón (1920–24) and in dialogue with the ideas of the minister of education, José Vasconcelos. It had strong ideological underpinnings that were rooted in national identity and Marxist political theories of class. The goal was to educate the masses and promote the vision of Mexico as a unified mestizo nation through images. The muralists challenged the idea of "art for art's sake" and developed an iconography featuring heroes from Mexico's past, present, and future—Aztec warriors battling the Spanish, peasants fighting in the Revolution, and urban workers from Mexico City.

The movement took shape around the work of three leading artists: Diego Rivera (1886–1957), David Alfaro Siqueiros (1896–1974), and José Clemente Orozco (1883–1949). Rivera's painting aligned most closely with the goals of the Revolution, while Orozco's belied a greater pessimism about the success of the decade-long conflict and the supposed realization of its goals, and Siqueiros's was more extreme in its expression of his radical political thinking. In conjunction with the Syndicate of Technical Workers, Painters, and Sculptors, of which both Rivera and Siqueiros were a part, Siqueiros penned the "Manifesto del Sindicato de Obreros Técnicas Pintores y Escultores." Published in the union's newspaper, *El Machete*, in 1924, the text, among other things, explained the aesthetic and ideological goals of Mexican muralism to socialize art.

Indigenist Art, Nativism
(El *arte indigenista*, El *indigenismo*)

Indigenismo (also referred to as Nativism), or Indigenist art, was an avant-garde movement developed in the late 1920s and 1930s by intellectuals and artists who wanted to counter the dominance of European art by celebrating Latin America's Indigenous past and looking for inspiration from pre-Columbian art traditions. Painters from Mexico, Bolivia, Brazil, Ecuador, and Peru produced their own style of *indigenista* art, as the historical subjects and ideological positions varied from country to country. The Andean *indigenista* movement was directly influenced by the work of the Mexican muralists (Rivera, Orozco, and Siqueiros), who unabashedly represented the Aztec legacy on their large-scale public murals and used Indigenous and mestizo subjects to convey the struggle of socialism against capitalism. In Ecuador, the mestizo artist Oswaldo Guayasamín (1919–99) painted expressive Indigenous, mestizo, and Black subjects to bring attention to social marginalization and political oppression. In the Andean countries of Peru and Bolivia, *indigenista* art was less politicized and tended to depict the native rural population with a focus on local festivals, landscapes, and ancestral traditions. Artists such as José Sabogal (1888–1956), a Peruvian of Spanish descent, painted Indigenous subjects to celebrate pre-Columbian culture and to create a symbol of national identity. Under Sabogal's direction (1932–43), Peru's National School of Fine Arts produced a variety of artists whose *indigenista* work had an archaeological rather than a political or social focus on their Indigenous subjects.

It is important to note the difference between the terms "Indigenous" (wherein the artwork is created by artists of Indigenous descent) and "Indigenist" (which refers to artwork created by artists who are not themselves Indigenous but who depict Indigenous peoples or cultures with an ancestral lens). The Ecuadorian artist Oswaldo Guayasamín, a mestizo, is considered an Indigenous artist, whereas José Sabogal is considered an Indigenist painter due to his lack of Indigenous heritage and the way Indian subjects are portrayed in his artwork. Indeed, the *indigenista* movement founded by Sabogal in Peru has been criticized as an attempt to "other" and simplify the large Indigenous populations who inhabit the Andean region.

Abstract Expressionism
(El *expresionismo abstracto*)

Abstract expressionism refers to an artistic movement that developed in the United States in the wake of World War II. The paintings of Jackson Pollock and Mark Rothko are two different pillars of this type of abstraction of the 1940s and 1950s. Pollock's gestural abstraction was defined by mark making and improvisation, whereas Rothko's color field paintings were defined by monochromatic areas of color. Abstract expressionism was the first avant-garde movement in the United States to gain international acclaim. While abstract expressionists did not all adhere to the same style, the term is associated with artists who shared a common existential view of the world and desire to convey emotion through formal means (such as line or color). These artists challenged traditional methods of painting through method and material. For example, Pollock notoriously laid his canvas on the ground and dripped house paint on it in a way that reflected the movement of his body's gestures. Abstract expressionism is sometimes referred to as the New York School to differentiate it from other modes of abstraction that developed on the West Coast. During the Cold War, the United States promoted abstract expressionism around the world, partly as a form of individual expression to counter Soviet Russia's official style of socialist realism. The Chilean artist Roberto Matta was considered a mentor to many of the New York abstract expressionists.

In Latin America, abstraction was highly contested, particularly in places like Peru and Mexico with strong pre-Columbian roots. Many artists began to reevaluate formal solutions to address their cultural concerns and their participation on an international platform. Artists like Bolivian painter María Luisa Pacheco (1919–82), who moved to New York City in 1956, was inspired by abstract expressionism, but like most Latin American artists, Pacheco did not model her own work after it. Instead, many Latin American artists were more aligned with the European postwar equivalent, Art Informel.

Art Informel did not adhere to any ideology or formal structures, allowing artists to explore gestural experimentations with a variety of materials. These explorations initiated Informalismo in Latin America, which opened the field to textural abstractions. The Peruvian artist Fernando de Szyszlo (1925–2017) was one of the first to adapt abstraction in Peru in the 1950s. De Szyszlo applied a range of color tones and impasto textures for a tactile quality on his canvases. At the same time, he imbued his work with Indigenous symbolism by employing colors and forms that are prominent in Inca art and titling his work after Inca subjects. In negotiating his interest in pre-Columbian art and the formal qualities of Informalismo, de Szyszlo achieved a synthesis of abstraction and a native aesthetic.

New York–born Puerto Rican artist Soraida Martinez (b. 1956) created her own distinct form of hard-edged abstract expressionism wherein paintings are juxtaposed with written social commentaries. Created in 1992 as a response to the diminishment of artistic accomplishments of Puerto Ricans, African Americans, women, and other minority groups, Verdadism consists of two distinct yet integral parts: the visual component and the written commentary. The visual style of Verdadism extends the boundaries of conventional abstract expressionism toward a more contemporary, multicultural perspective where broad areas of bold colors and geometric shapes coalesce and synthesize to create a harmonious composition. And although much of the visual aspect of Verdadism emphasizes hard-edge abstraction, stylistically speaking it also reveals the spiritual influence of the art of many periods and cultures—including "naïve" principles, elements of surrealism, and West African sculpture.

Chicano Art (El arte chicano)

In the late 1960s and early 1970s, identity politics became a significant issue in the visual arts. The Chicano movement, centered in California, was one of the civil rights movements that developed in these years. It is a political and cultural movement led by predominantly working-class Americans of Mexican descent. Chicano/a artists sought to combat pervasive, often negative stereotypes of Latinos/as and to take ownership of how their own identities as Mexican Americans were represented. Through the frequent use of popular imagery, Chicano/a artists reassessed their cultural heritage. The movement is known for its use of public space and serial production. Through photography, graphic arts, murals, and architectural installation, artists sought to reach those living within their communities and beyond.

The movement was not one-dimensional, and various Chicano/a artists challenged different aspects of mainstream representation of their identities as artists and as self-identified Chicano/as. The first Chicano art gallery opened in 1969 in East Los Angeles. The collective Los Four (The Four)—Carlos Almarez, Frank Romero, Beto de la Rocha, and Gilbert Lujan—was formed in the 1970s. The group exhibited collectively and collaboratively made murals.

Asco (1972–87) was a Chicano performance and conceptual art collective that saw itself in opposition to some parts of the Chicano art movement, yet each member identified as Chicano/a and fought for representation in official venues. The group's motto, "By any means necessary," defined their practice and activism as they worked across mediums such as performance and photography.

Portrait of the Artist as the Virgin of Guadalupe, by Yolanda López (1942–2021), is a notable example of Chicana art in that she plays off of the iconic image of the Virgin of Guadalupe. She inserts herself in place of the Virgin, striding toward the viewer with a mantle decorated with stars draped over her shoulder. The series consists of three portraits; the other two represent her mother and grandmother. These works are notable in that they use iconic, popular imagery to reevaluate representations of their cultural heritage and women. The movement has continued to evolve over time, further integrating other layers of identity politics such as gender and sexuality in the twenty-first century.

Latin American Street Art (*El arte callejero*)

Street art came to challenge the commercialization of art internationally. In Latin America, it arose in reaction to political turmoil. It thus shares parallels, and at times overlaps, with performance art and other modes of political or activist art. Street art, however, often more narrowly refers to graffiti or other forms of graphic arts like wheatpasting in public spaces. But whereas modern-day graffiti revolves around tagging and text-based subject matter, street art is more open and usually more explicitly political. Common materials and techniques include flyposting, stenciling, stickers, freehand drawing, and projected videos. It is not a cohesive movement or style. Many street artists have navigated between the streets, studios, and gallery or museum exhibitions.

While graffiti art began in New York City in the 1970s, in Latin America, a number of artists developed their own styles. For instance, Os Gemeos (The Twins)—a Brazilian duo—began creating street art in the late 1980s. The twin brothers have used house paint, rollers, and brushes to cover public walls with surreal imagery that responds to their environment.

In public spaces throughout Latin America, street art represents the voice of the community, marginalized groups, and young people who strive to be heard, often challenging the concept of private property. For example, in Chile groups like CADA (Colectivo de Acciones de Arte) used public space to stage actions such as *No +* (No more). This project consisted of posting the statement *No +* in public space as an invitation for participation, beginning in 1983. The public could then fill in its discontent under the dictatorship of Augusto Pinochet (1973–90). This action was performative, participatory, and graphic. Another example is the Street Art Group (Grupo de Arte Callejero, GAC) from Argentina. Throughout the 1960s and 1970s, the country experienced a series of violent military regimes that repressed individual freedom and the right to free speech. After Argentina's return to democracy in 1983, and in response to the catastrophic economic crisis of the 1990s, GAC used the streets of Buenos Aires as their canvas for public dissent.

Hyperrealism (*El hiperrealismo*)

Hyperrealism (not to be confused here with photorealism) emerged in the late twentieth century, developing out of the American photorealism movement, which became popular in the 1970s by creating extraordinarily realistic-looking paintings based on photographic images. The earlier movement of photorealism began as a response to the nonfigurative and nonrepresentational art of abstract expressionism, which eschewed realistic depictions of their subjects on the canvas. Photorealist artists project a photographic image onto the canvas, divide it into an intricate grid system, and then incorporate elements of high-resolution photography such as depth of field and reflections to create the illusion of a photographic image through painting. Hyperrealist artists also begin with photographic images, usually taken by the artists themselves with professional-grade digital cameras, and then re-create the image on canvas. Despite the high degree of skill, craftsmanship, and technical precision needed to create the sharply photographic images that characterize photorealism and hyperrealism, some art critics have disparaged the artist's dependence on a photographic image and perceived lack of originality. The 1980 exhibition *Realism and Latin American Painting* brought together a group of twelve artists, mostly from Colombia, who were creating artwork in the photorealist mode.

Twenty-first-century hyperrealism is considered an advancement of the techniques popularized by photorealism, made possible by higher-resolution photography and innovations in camera technology. Whereas photorealist paintings maintain a strict fealty to the objective re-creation of a photographic image, hyperrealist paintings from the 2000s tend to incorporate social or political themes. The Cuban artist Joel Corrales Márquez, for example, transforms his hyperrealist depictions of everyday Cubans (based on photographs from the streets of Havana) into sleeping giants who lie across crumbling buildings, infusing his paintings with messages about globalization and poverty. Paul Cadden, a renowned hyperrealist painter, has clarified that twenty-first-century hyperrealism is not simply about representing reality in a literal fashion through a new medium, as was the case with 1970s photorealism. Rather, hyperrealism is about infusing a lifelike, realistic appearance with emotional, social, cultural, and political themes. In this sense, the latest iteration of hyperrealism calls attention to the postmodern idea of simulated reality and the role of digital media in creating a new sense of reality.

Naïve or Naïf Art
(El arte primitivo, El arte naíf)

The term "naïve art" refers to works by self-taught artists who do not look to the history of art as a point of reference. Their work is often characterized as unsophisticated, as they do not have formal training (in anatomy, technique, and perspective) or adhere to academic standards of representation. The category of naïve art has origins in the arts and crafts of rural peoples, more often referred to as folk art. During the nineteenth century, with the rise of industrialization and a decline in folk art production, the determination of unschooled artists began to gain attention. A framework to appreciate naïve art had long been established through the early writings of philosopher Jean-Jacques Rousseau, who praised the virtues of the "noble savage." By the turn of the century, modern artists celebrated naïve art for its sincere expression that is not bound to any artistic traditions.

The most prominent figure to arise during the modern period is Henri Rousseau (1844–1910), who became known for his imaginary jungle scenes. He meticulously rendered the minutiae of foliage with no regard for natural imperfections, proportions, or perspective. Rousseau captured the attention of many avant-garde figures, and by 1886 he exhibited with the juryless Société des Artistes Indépendants, where his work was displayed alongside modern artists such as Seurat, Signac, and Redon. In the United States, Anna Mary Robertson Moses, known as Grandma Moses (1860–1961), is a distinguished example of a naïve artist who worked from memory, often reflecting on the local landscape and activities of everyday life.

In nineteenth-century Latin America, art academies were few and limited to the major capitals, leaving many artists in small towns with no access to academic training in the arts. Nonetheless, local self-taught artists fulfilled the need to document or narrate secular and religious events. Portraiture also had a long-standing tradition. In Mexico, Hermenegildo Bustos (1832–1907) is one of the most celebrated examples of an accomplished autodidact, known for his portraiture. The work of José Antonio Velásquez (1906–83) from Honduras is a mix of naïve and folk art. His whimsical interpretations of rural life resulted in romanticized landscapes that are highly sought after by a tourist market.

The category of naïve art continues to encompass wide-ranging aesthetic and formal qualities that are identified with many works within the larger field of outsider art (*art brut*, in French)—a field of art production considered outside the Western canon. Characterized by childlike simplicity of execution, naïve painting can be recognized by its refusal to incorporate formal qualities of painting, especially the rejection of these three rules of perspective: (1) decrease of the size of objects proportionally with distance, (2) muting of colors with distance, and (3) decrease of the precision of details with distance. As a result, naïve paintings create effects of perspective that are geometrically erroneous, and apply equal accuracy to details, including those of the background, which should be shaded off.

3

The Game

WHAT IS LATIN AMERICAN ART?

The art produced before the conquest?

The art created during the three-hundred-year
colonial period?

The art of the post-independence era?

Popular art, a product of the backwardness and
poverty of large sectors or our population?

Cultured academic art of the nineteenth century?

Could our culture exist without Greece or Rome?

Can we deny the Christian influence on the art of
Roman Catholic countries?

Have not the black people on our continent
contributed their own sensibility?

Has the cultural imperialism of this century
altered our traditions?

Have we not had East Asian influences since the
beginning of our civilization?

All of the above means only that we are peoples
with a great cultural heritage, and faced with
the impossibility of reducing it to one, single
product, we must accept that our art is a plural
and highly diverse expression.

—Manuel Felguérez, quoted in Frank, *Manifestos and
Polemics in Latin American Modern Art*

If you read the game materials and your individual
role sheet carefully, you should be well prepared.
The debates fall into two main categories: (1) "What
is Latin American art?" and (2) "Latin American art
in the world today." The following resources are
essential for understanding the issues at stake and
playing the game:

- Chapter 2 (Historical Background) provides
  the broad context for the issues.
- Chapter 3 (The Game) provides details about
  major debate topics, as well as strategies and tips
  for playing the game, including the blank canvas
  points, voting mechanics, rules, procedures, and
  individual game sessions.

- Chapter 5 (Core Texts) introduces the main artistic and ideological frameworks.
- Your role sheet details your background, position, and specific goals or objectives.
- The role sheet and bibliography suggest extra readings to deepen your understanding.

Latin America is a complex, multifaceted region, so there are many things to consider when creating an exhibit with a diverse representation of Latin American art. *The Prado Museum Expansion* provides an opportunity to view, analyze, and debate a range of artistic movements and styles related to Latin American art throughout the twentieth century. In addition, we will discuss the role and changing identity of Latin American art as it enters the twenty-first century. Indeed, in order to understand Latin American art in 2010 (the year of the game), we must look back at the artwork and artists that defined this concept throughout the twentieth century. For this reason, the first debate session ("What Is Latin American Art?") will be led by the art dealers representing the deceased artists whose artwork helped define our current understanding of Latin American art. As experts in the wide variety of styles that shaped the work of Diego Rivera, Joaquín Torres García, Oswaldo Guayasamín, Wifredo Lam, Roberto Matta, Frida Kahlo, Xul Solar, Tarsila do Amaral, Remedios Varo, and José Sabogal, the art dealers will debate the importance of the European avant-garde, the colonial legacy of Spain and Portugal, and the role of national identity in twentieth-century Latin American art. In the subsequent session ("Latin American Art in the World Today"), the next generation of artists will lead the discussion about new ways of thinking about their artwork in a globalized and changing world. These artists have much to say about issues of gender, race, ethnicity, politics, and the role of museums in the twenty-first century.

Each individual involved in the negotiations will bring a unique perspective and their own beliefs regarding these issues. The following are the major topics that will be debated. You should read them carefully and think about your character's stance on these issues. You are encouraged to incorporate some of these topics into your speech, citing the related core texts where relevant.

What Is Latin American Art?— Debate Topics

Latin America is comprised of many different countries, peoples, and cultures. Who is included under the umbrella of "Latin American art"? What makes the art of Latin America unique? What should be represented in the artwork to best give visitors of the Prado Museum a grasp of Latin American culture? How can different artworks create the fabric of a narrative that depicts differences woven together in one big picture? Which paintings will give a diverse and accurate representation of the history of twentieth-century Latin American art? During the session "What Is Latin American Art?," the art dealers will present their opinions on the following major issues in a formal speech. The curators and artists should be prepared to ask follow-up questions related to these big ideas.

Latin American Art and the European Avant-Garde

- What are the major "isms" that emerged during the 1920s–40s as part of the European avant-garde? How did they influence Latin American artists during this time period?
- What are some of the similarities and differences between some of these artistic movements and styles?
- How did artists from Latin America influence, adapt and modify European artistic styles such as cubism, surrealism, constructivism, and expressionism?

The Encounter of Different Worlds

- The colonial legacy of Spain and Portugal forcibly shaped the languages, societal structures, governance, traditions, and religions of Latin America. How does Latin American art represent and resist the history of colonialization by Spain and Portugal?
- What role does art play in remembering and representing the many and diverse Indigenous cultures that make Latin America unique?
- How did African cultures influence Latin American art? Why is this important?
- Who has the right to represent Indigenous or Afro-descendant subjects on canvas?

National, Regional, or International?

- Should diversity be defined along geographic and national boundaries to ensure that most, if not all, countries in Latin America are represented in the new gallery? Why is this important?
- What are some of the reasons for defining an artist as "international" or "global," as opposed to "Chilean" or "Latin American"? What is your view on cosmopolitanism vs. nationalism in the context of Latin American art?
- How does a national or regional identity help a museum audience understand a particular piece of art? What are the advantages and disadvantages of this classification?

Latin American Art and the World Today— Debate Topics

What is the place of Latin American art in the global art world today? What does diversity in art mean? Recently the term "Latin American art" has been called into question by art critics and curators as a limiting and simplistic approach to contemporary art. Indeed, the very label "Latin America" is a colonial concept that privileges a Euro-dominant perspective. Has the moment arrived to change this master narrative? What new innovations are possible when artists from Argentina, Brazil, Chile, Costa Rica, Colombia, Cuba, the US-Mexico border, and Puerto Rico are empowered to guide the development of global art? During Session 6 ("Latin American Art and the World Today") the artists will present their opinions on the following major issues in a formal speech. The curators and art dealers should be prepared to ask follow-up questions related to these big ideas.

Gender and Race

- What role do female artists play in the world of Latin American art? Why should this be taken into consideration for the exhibit?
- What is the racial and ethnic composition of Latin America? How do particular artworks reflect this reality?
- Should the artists selected for the exhibit embody a diverse representation of gender, race, and ethnicity? Why or why not?
- How has Latin American art addressed issues of race and gender? Has this changed over time?

Art as Politics

- How do particular pieces of art add to an understanding of the different cultures, languages, and peoples of Latin America?
- What are some of the limitations of the label "Latin American art"?
- How does your artwork address notions of power and representation?
- What are some differences between art that innovates through form/technique and art that depicts politics or a political position through its content?
- What are the advantages and disadvantages of selecting "art for art's sake"? Should art be selected and enjoyed solely for aesthetic purposes?
- Where can contemporary art find a diverse audience? How can a piece of art influence the thoughts and actions of its viewers?

The Future of Museums

- Who will be coming to the Prado to see this exhibit and why?
- What message does the art send to the viewers? How does this reflect on the Prado's particular history as a purveyor of art in Europe?
- Are there new modalities of creating, displaying, and viewing art that require museums to adapt their traditional forms of art exhibition and curation? Is the Prado prepared to make these changes?

RULES AND PROCEDURES

This game is designed as an art competition that brings together living artists and art dealers from Latin America as they compete for a coveted place in the Prado's new gallery. Museum restrictions on space, rather than budget, is what drives the competition. Only a limited number of paintings (roughly half of those submitted for consideration) will be selected for the new exhibit space. If an artist's or art dealer's painting is not chosen for the gallery, they lose the game. The curators (with help from the patron of the arts, private collector, and marketing director) decide which paintings will be chosen for the new gallery. If the curators are unable, for any reason, to secure the required number of paintings, the Prado Museum administration will rescind their curatorial duties and cancel the permanent gallery. Of course, each individual player may also have specific and/or private victory objectives they must work hard to achieve before time runs out!

Objectives, Victory Conditions, and Voting

The primary objective for the majority of the artists and art dealers is to ensure that their painting is selected for the Prado's new gallery. They should work hard to convince the curators of the merits (aesthetic, historical, ideological) of their artwork. The artists and art dealers have a secondary victory objective that is related to their careers after the Prado competition. Most of the living artists are looking to sign a contract with an art dealer to ensure a successful future career. Artists and art dealers should read their individual role sheet and the assigned sections of the game book carefully and prepare the necessary information before each session. It is your responsibility to come prepared for each game session. The curators are your guides in this process. You should approach them, rather than the game manager (GM), first to ask any questions you have. For art dealers and living artists, one of your most important tasks is to bring your painting in color to every session. You may bring a reprint, print it out yourself (oversized printer, Staples, etc.),

TABLE 3 Vote distribution for painting competition

No. of paintings in competition	Gallery spots*	Best speech (art dealer)	Best speech (artist)	Curators	Duque	Private collector
20 (option A)	11	2	2	3	2	2
20 (option B)	10	1	1	4	2	2
18–19	9	1	1	3	2	2
16–17	8	1	1	4	1	1
14–15	7	1	1	3	1	1
11–13	6	1	1	2	1	1
8–10	5	*	*	2	1	1
Session revealed		6	6	7	7	7

*If there are only five gallery spots, the winners of the best speech by an art dealer and an artist move to a runoff vote in Session 6 to determine which painting will be given a spot in the gallery.

or re-create it by hand (the bigger, the better!). In some instances, the GM may prefer to have digital versions of the artwork. In any case, this is your chance to win over the curators with an impressive painting.

While additional victory objectives are present for all characters in the game, none of them can be achieved without interacting and talking to one another in the course of the game. No one will win without engaging with the other characters in the context of the game. Ask questions, listen to speeches, and seek out other characters in order to achieve the outlined victory objectives in your role sheet.

Voting Mechanics

There should be a balance of artworks between those paintings submitted by art dealers and those submitted by living artists in the competition. The total number of paintings for the new gallery should be approximately half as many as the number of paintings submitted to the competition. Use table 3 to calculate how the votes are distributed, based on how many paintings are entered in the competition. *Note:* Although this circumstance is highly unusual, some artists and art dealers may decline to show at the Prado. If an artist or art dealer declines the offer, the curators will choose the replacement from

among the individuals with the most blank canvas points.

Voting Schedule

After the formal speeches in Session 5 ("What Is Latin American Art?"), there will be a closed ballot vote by the living artists to determine the best speech by an art dealer. This represents a guaranteed spot in the Prado gallery. However, curators will communicate the results privately to the GM.

Voting continues in Session 6 ("Latin American Art and the World Today") in this order:

1. After the formal speeches, there will be a closed ballot vote by the art dealers to determine the best speech by a living artist. This represents a guaranteed spot in the Prado gallery.
2. At the end of this session, the results for best speech by an art dealer and a living artist will be announced. If there is a need for a run-off vote (e.g., only five gallery spots are available), then the artists and art dealers vote to determine which of the "best speech" nominees will be offered a spot in the Prado. In the event of any ties, curators will prioritize the artist or art dealer with the most blank canvas points at that point in the game.

3. After this session, curators independently make one selection each (cannot be the winner of the best speech) for the gallery. If curators are required to select a total of three or more paintings, they will jointly decide on the remaining paintings (refer to table 3 above). Curators must communicate their choices to the GM privately after Session 6. Their preferred selections will not be announced until Session 7 ("Gallery Decisions"). All remaining gallery selections will be determined during the gallery decisions session.

During Session 7, gallery decisions will be announced in the following manner:

1. At the beginning of this session, the curators will announce the paintings that have a guaranteed spot in the gallery based on the best speech results. These paintings should be displayed prominently at the front of the room.
2. After the speed manifestos (and any last-minute negotiations), the patron of the arts and private collector each announce their selections for the Prado. If either of these pieces has already been selected or if the patron's or private collector's vote is forfeited, the curators will consult with the GM about game protocol.
3. In the event of forfeiture or insufficient blank canvas points, the curators will select any remaining works to be included in the gallery, in consultation with the marketing director. The decisions must bring the total number of paintings to approximately 50 percent of the original number of artists and art dealers in the competition. Curators should make their decisions from the pool of remaining artists and art dealers with the most blank canvas points.

Blank Canvas Points
Each invited artist and art dealer will create a digital blank canvas (fig. 1) that will help determine your influence and status within the art world. Players who work hard to earn blank canvas points will in turn benefit from wider visibility within the game.

You can obtain blank canvas points for the successful completion of any of the activities and tasks listed in the "How to Earn Points" section. In addition, you may propose alternative tasks or activities to the GM for consideration. You must have at least 10 points (from at least two different color categories) by the end of Session 4 ("Gallery Walk") to be considered for inclusion in the exhibit.

As you complete these activities, document each one on a digital or physical canvas (for example, a shared Google doc or a piece of paper) and ask the docent or GM to "approve" them by painting the relevant color and points on your blank canvas. The docent may ask you to provide evidence of the activity (for example, a photo, video, artifact, testimony from other players, social media posts, written submissions). If possible, this evidence should be attached to your blank canvas. In some cases, you may not know if you have received the points until the last game session (e.g., appearance in the marketing director's video or publication of your submission in *Círculo y Cuadrado*). You are encouraged to try to obtain as many blank canvas points as possible. More experience yields greater influence and fame in the art world.

For artists: For every 10 blank canvas points you earn beyond the basic requirement of 10 points by the end of the gallery walk session, you can add one condition to your contract with an art dealer.

For art dealers: For every 10 blank canvas points you earn beyond the basic requirement of 10 points by the end of the gallery walk session, you can add one condition to your contract with a living artist.

Do You Have Your Own Blank Canvas Ideas?
The art world embraces CREATIVITY! Feel free to come up with your own blank canvas ideas related to art and/or Latin America. Remember to ask Martín Romero (docent) or the GM for approval and point distribution.

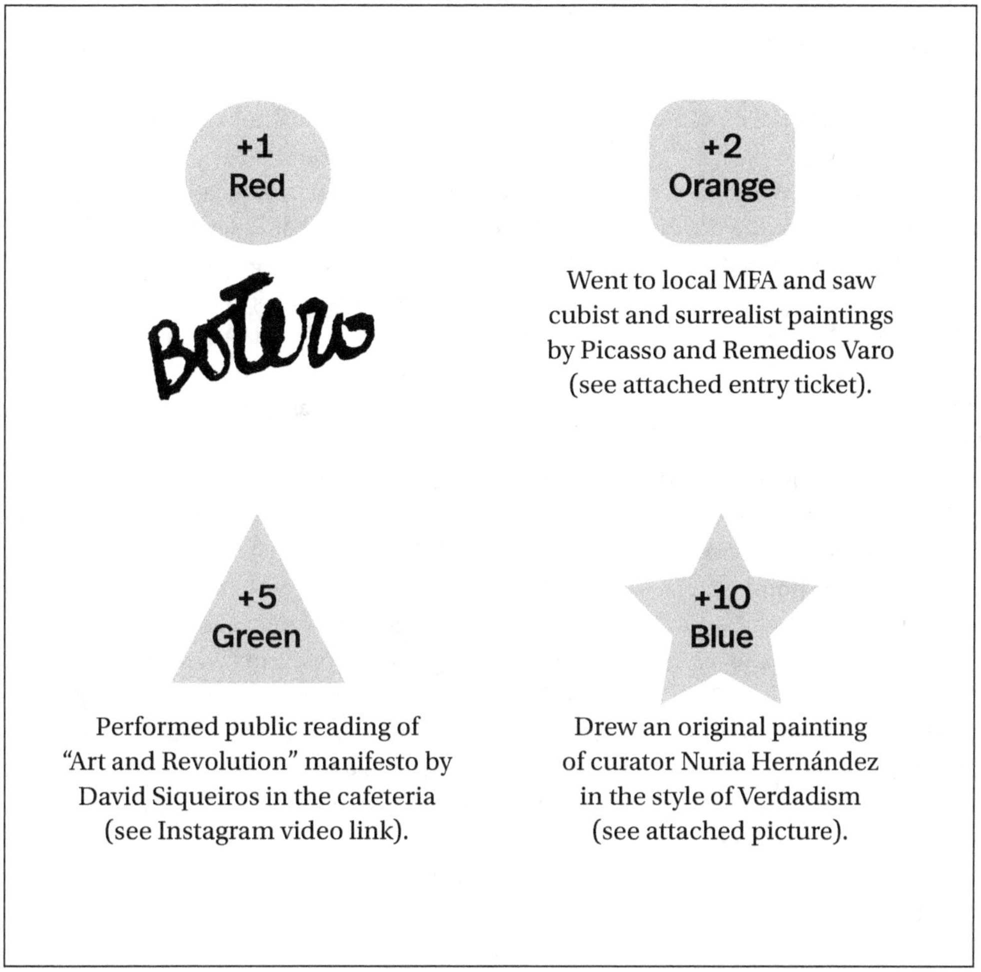

FIGURE 1
Sample blank
canvas

+1
Red

BOTERO

+2
Orange

Went to local MFA and saw
cubist and surrealist paintings
by Picasso and Remedios Varo
(see attached entry ticket).

+5
Green

+10
Blue

Performed public reading of
"Art and Revolution" manifesto by
David Siqueiros in the cafeteria
(see Instagram video link).

Drew an original painting
of curator Nuria Hernández
in the style of Verdadism
(see attached picture).

How to Earn Points

Red (1 point)

- Create a pin of your country's flag and wear it
  during the game sessions.
- Wear a costume or bring a prop that reflects
  your character.
- Wear jewelry or clothing that reflects your
  cultural heritage or artistic style.
- Wear the colors of your country's flag or bring
  your national flag to any session.
- Learn how to say "painting" and/or "art" in
  Spanish, Portuguese, Quechua, and Mayan (or
  another Indigenous language from the region).
- Learn a colloquial greeting in your artist's or
  art dealer's country's native language(s) and
  use it to greet other players.
- Learn how to forge your artist's signature and
  sign it on your blank canvas.
- Attend a game session wearing clothes that are
  all the same color, and explain the sensory significance of the color to as many other players
  as possible.

Orange (2 points)

- Create a mini version of your artwork on a pin or sticker and distribute to other players.
- Post an image of your artwork on social media and receive at least five "likes."
- Ask another player to define the artistic style/movement of your painting, based on the definitions in the game book (write their answer on your blank canvas).
- Listen to a podcast about Latin American art and write a paragraph response.
- Send an email or written note (in character) to another player in the game. The communication must demonstrate meaningful engagement with the game (e.g., references to a core text or questions about a specific piece of art or game concept). Copy the GM on your correspondence.
- Create a pamphlet or flyer containing information about your artist, art movement, and/or ideology and distribute to players.
- Bring a color print version of your painting, with dimensions larger than 8.5 by 11 inches, to any session.
- Visit a local museum and identify at least two different artistic styles represented. Include images of the artwork (this can be a virtual/digital or in-person visit).
- Ask an artist or art dealer to describe your painting using four different adjectives (write these on your blank canvas with the artist/art dealer's name).
- Your name or painting is mentioned or shown in Isadora López's marketing video (or in another character's marketing/publicity video).

Green (5 points)

- Perform a public reading of a Latin American artist's manifesto.
- Draw a rendition of the Prado Museum using one of the avant-garde styles.
- Write a song or poem in Spanish or Portuguese that expresses your artist's ideas.
- Use a quote from one of the artists' interviews in the core texts in your speech.
- Find an interview with a curator of an exhibit about Latin American art and summarize the curator's vision in a paragraph.
- Bring refreshments from your country or culture to one of the game sessions.
- Watch the documentary *Waste Land* and submit a film review to the journal *Círculo y Cuadrado*.
- Watch a film related to art in the Spanish-speaking world (verify relevance with GM) and submit a film review to *Círculo y Cuadrado*.
- Submit an entry (visual, text) to *Círculo y Cuadrado* (the entry must be accepted and published by Sr. Garza or your blank canvas points will be rescinded during the gallery decisions session).
- Ask all three of your prepared questions during Session 5 ("What Is Latin American Art") or 6 ("Latin American Art and the World Today"). Record the responses on your canvas as evidence.
- Interview a local museum curator about how he or she makes decisions for new exhibitions.
- Visit a museum or exhibit (virtually or in-person) with artwork by Latino or Latin American artists and submit a report to the marketing director with possible ideas for the Prado gallery.
- Ask Vik Muniz about his work with the *catadores* and gift him a piece of art using recycled materials.
- Your voice (in the form of a quote, voice-over, or interview segment) appears in Isadora López's marketing video (or in another character's marketing/publicity video).

Blue (10 points)

- Organize and run a *taller* (workshop) on painting.
- Create an original painting in the style of your artist.
- Recruit three people (not in the game) to attend Session 7 ("Gallery Decisions") and to try to influence the curators, patron of the arts, and private collector to pick your painting.
- Based on the guidelines in "How to Paint a Mural," create a mural in the classroom or on campus (don't violate campus rules!—this may need to be a temporary mural, performance piece, or other public art installation in/outside of the classroom).
- Create your own hype video, highlighting the important aspects of your artwork. You are encouraged to include other players in the video, as relevant (alliance-building!), and to post the video to social media.
- Organize a film screening of a documentary or docudrama about any of the artists in the competition (living or deceased) and moderate a Q&A afterward.
- Organize and perform a short play about your artist's beliefs and cultural background.
- Contact a living Latin American artist and ask them questions about their art and style, then record the responses on your blank canvas and submit the interview to the docent.
- Group three or four paintings according to a theme and organize a "Call and Response" for which anyone can submit their own original work that responds in some way to the theme.

BASIC OUTLINE OF THE GAME

The Prado Museum Expansion begins with two (or more) preparatory sessions to get you ready for Reacting to the Past and to introduce some of the skills and concepts you will need to analyze formal elements of art and to talk about Latin American art. The next five game sessions are followed by one final debrief session about your *Prado* game experience, for a total of eight sessions. Depending on your class needs and objectives, the GM may add or compress this game session schedule.

En español: If you are playing the game in Spanish, sessions might be added to introduce new vocabulary, help with library research in Spanish, practice your public speeches, and work on essay writing. These sessions will be scheduled at your instructor's discretion.

Preparatory Sessions
Session 1: Introduction to Reacting to the Past
Session 1 is a preparatory session to familiarize players with Reacting to the Past (RTTP) pedagogy. You will also learn more about how the *Prado* game works. All players will be assigned an individual role immediately before or at the close of today's session, but you are not expected to come to the session "in character" yet. You should have this game book before Session 1 in order to read the assigned sections carefully, bring your questions and be prepared for a quiz (optional) on the assigned readings. The game can seem overwhelming at first glance, so remember to pace yourself and prepare one session at a time. Jumping ahead or trying to figure everything out at once is unnecessary and will most likely make your experience in the game more confusing.

REQUIRED READINGS

Read before coming to class today:

- Chapter 1: Introduction (all sections)
- Chapter 2: Historical Background ("The Art World": all subsections); and
- Chapter 3: The Game ("Major Issues for Debate"; "Rules and Procedures": [all subsections]; "Basic Outline of the Game": Session 1 ["Introduction to Reacting to the Past"])

ACTIVITIES (MAY VARY ACCORDING TO INSTRUCTOR)

- Introduction to RTTP
- You will be assigned a role and you will receive an individual role sheet before or during today's session (*the role sheets are private and must be kept confidential throughout the game play*)
- Q&A session about RTTP and *Prado* game.
- Quiz on assigned readings (optional; GM will decide if quiz is administered during or after today's session).

Session 2: Introduction to Latin American Art

In Session 2, the GM will introduce you to a chronological history of twentieth-century Latin American art, with a focus on the following artistic movements and styles: expressionism, cubism, surrealism, constructivism, abstract expressionism, hyperrealism, muralism, Indigenist art, naïve art, and street art. Although you are still not expected to be "in character" for this preparatory session, you should begin to think about how your character fits (or not) into this context. There will be a discussion about different ways to define Latin American art and the complexities of such an endeavor. You should study the assigned readings carefully, bring any questions, and be prepared for a quiz (optional) on the information in the "Artistic Movements and Styles" section of Chapter 2: Historical Background.

REQUIRED READINGS

Read before coming to class today:

- Chapter 2: Historical Background ("Artistic Movements and Styles": all sections and table 2)
- Chapter 3: The Game ("Basic Outline of the Game": Session 2 ["Introduction to Latin American Art"])
- Chapter 5: Core Texts (Damián Bayón, "When Will the Art of Latin America Become Latin American Art?"; "The Identity of Contemporary Latin American Art"; and "An Interview with Oswaldo Guayasamín")
- Carefully read your individual role sheet

ASSIGNMENTS DUE

- **All players**: Complete Pregame Discussion Questions (see Chapter 3: The Game: "Assignments and Templates")

ACTIVITIES (MAY VARY ACCORDING TO INSTRUCTOR)

- Review of Chapter 2: Historical Background ("Artistic Movements and Styles") with representative paintings
- Discussion about Latin American art
- Quiz on assigned readings (optional; GM will decide whether quiz is administered during or after today's session)

Game Sessions

Session 3: Welcome to the Prado

The *Prado* game begins! All players should come to today's session in character with their painting (as relevant) and any other props. You will be welcomed to the Prado Museum in Madrid, Spain, by the curators, Nuria Hernández and Roberto Pérez, and the museum docent, Martín Romero. After setting up their artworks around the gallery space, the living artists and the art dealers who represent deceased Latin American artists will have an opportunity to briefly introduce themselves. We will also hear from the patron of the arts (el Duque de Artega) and the private art collector (Sr. Lustres). Today's session will include a discussion about the Major Issues for Debate, and there will be some open time to get to know one another better, earn blank canvas points, and network with the Prado Museum staff and supporters.

REQUIRED READINGS
Read before coming to class today:

- Chapter 3: The Game ("Basic Outline of the Game": Session 3 ["Welcome to the Prado"], including its discussion questions)
- Chapter 4: Roles and Factions ("Roles"; "Brief Outline of Each Role"; "Factions": "Geographic Factions")

ASSIGNMENTS DUE
- **All artists and art dealers** must submit their entry for the museum catalog today (see Chapter 3: The Game ["Assignments and Templates": "Catalog Entry"]). All artists and art dealers must also bring their artwork with them to this session and every session thereafter. The GM and/or the marketing director will specify if your catalog entry should be printed or submitted digitally.
- **Curators** will give their formal speeches, presenting context for the Prado Museum's new initiative as well as their particular vision for the new gallery of Latin American art. *Note:* The formal speech is the foundation for a written essay. The GM will provide guidance about the length of the speech and how this assignment will be evaluated, as well as the specific due date for the written essay.

ACTIVITIES
- Paintings will be organized around the gallery by geographic factions.
- Curators will give their formal speeches.
- After the curators present, the marketing director (Isadora López) and museum docent (Martín Romero) will explain their roles, the museum catalog, and the blank canvas activity. Next the curators will introduce the patron of the arts (el Duque de Artega) and the private art collector, Sr. Lustres. El Duque and Sr. Lustres will talk briefly about their interests (this is not their formal speech).
- Next, the artists and art dealers will introduce themselves: who they are, where they are from, the name of their painting, and any important details that other players should know (this is not their formal speech).
- The curators will guide an open discussion about some of the major issues to be debated (see discussion questions for this session below). Players can be divided into pairs or small groups to discuss and report back to larger group.
- In the remaining open time, players are encouraged to circulate and get to know one another better. You should ask questions about the artwork, as well as other characters' interests and their understanding of Latin American art. This information will be helpful as you think about alliances, potential conflicts of interest, and how to best achieve your own victory objectives. Artists and art dealers are also encouraged to use this time to earn blank canvas points, as they must have at least 10 points (from at least two different color categories) by the end of the next session to be considered for inclusion in the exhibit. Artists and art dealers with fewer than 10 blank canvas points by the end of Session 4 ("Gallery Walk") will be eliminated from the competition.

DISCUSSION QUESTIONS FOR SESSION 3
The curators will guide a discussion about some of the major issues that will come to the fore during our negotiations. As you know, Latin America comprises many different countries, peoples, and cultures. Who is included under the "Latin American art" umbrella? What makes the art of Latin America unique? To help us think through these ideas, here are some questions to get us started.

- Should the concept "The Diverse Art of Latin America" be defined along geographic or national boundaries to ensure that most countries in Latin America are represented in the new gallery? Why is this important or not important?
- What are some reasons for defining an artist as "international" or "global," as opposed to "Chilean," "Mexican," "Caribbean," or "Latin American"?
- How does a national (e.g., Mexican muralist) or regional (Caribbean painter) identity help a museum audience understand a particular piece of art? What are the advantages and disadvantages of these kinds of classifications for our gallery?
- How can individual pieces of visual art create the fabric of a narrative that depicts differences woven together in one big picture? What might be lost in this approach to the exhibition?
- Which subjects/topics/images should be represented in the new gallery to help visitors to the Prado Museum understand Latin American culture and history?
- Who will be coming to the Prado to see this exhibit and why? What message should the art send to the viewers? Are there new modalities of creating, displaying, and viewing art that require museums to adapt their traditional forms of art exhibition and curation?

Session 4: Gallery Walk

We are headed on a gallery walk at the museum today! After hearing from the Duque de Artega and Sr. Lustres about their particular visions for the new gallery, the curators will provide an overview of some of the formal aspects of visual art. Next, players will spend time performing close readings of the paintings in the Prado competition, as they pay attention to the formal aspects of art, such as shape, line, color, proportion, volume, and subject matter. Originally grouped by geographic regions in Latin America, artists and art dealers will reorganize into new factions based on artistic movement and style. There will also be time in today's session to negotiate with other players and work toward achieving game objectives.

REQUIRED READINGS

Read before coming to class today:

- Chapter 3: The Game ("Basic Outline of the Game": Session 4 ["Gallery Walk"], including its discussion questions)
- Chapter 4: Roles and Factions ("Artistic Factions")
- Chapter 5: Core Texts (Hermine Feinstein, "How to Read Art for Meaning"; Hermine Feinstein, "The Dimensions of Color"; and Gretchen K. McKay, Nicolas W. Proctor, and Michael A. Marlais, "How to Read a Visual Image")
- *Review* Chapter 2: Historical Background ("Artistic Movements and Styles"; table 2: "Chronology of Artistic Movements"). Artists and art dealers: Be prepared to summarize the main characteristics of your artistic movement(s) or style(s) to other players today.

ASSIGNMENTS DUE

- **El Duque de Artega and Sr. Lustres** will each give a formal speech about their aesthetic and ideological preferences. *Note:* The formal speech is the foundation for a written essay. The GM will provide guidance about the length of the speech and how this assignment will be evaluated, as well as the specific due date for the written essay.
- **Curators** will prepare a brief presentation about the formal characteristics of painting based on today's core texts readings.
- **Artists and art dealers** should complete the "Gallery Walk" sheet for their own painting before coming to class today (see Chapter 3: The Game ["Assignments and Templates"]). The GM will provide a blank "Gallery Walk" sheet for all players during today's session.
- **The marketing director, in collaboration with the docent**, will distribute the museum catalog to all players (digital or print version).

ACTIVITIES

- Curators welcome everyone back and invite el Duque and Sr. Lustres to give their speeches. Artists and art dealers are expected to respond to el Duque and Sr. Lustres with questions and comments about their speeches.
- Curators will give a brief presentation about the formal characteristics of painting, followed by the gallery walk, in which all players select a painting of their choice (artists and art dealers should not select their own artwork). After the gallery walk, the curators will invite players to share their observations with the larger group and seek out individual artists or art dealers to ask specific questions about the paintings.
- At some point during this session, artists and art dealers will reorganize themselves according to their artistic factions, and each group will be expected to prepare a short summary of the main characteristics of their artistic movement or style faction (see discussion questions below). *Note:* Indeterminate (independent) players may place themselves in one or more of these categories (they must be able to explain why they belong to or were influenced by a particular movement or style) or may opt to remain independent. If you remain indeterminate, you must explain why.
- There will be some open time for blank canvas activities and discussions. All artists and art dealers must have at least 10 points (from at least two different color categories) by the end of today's session to be considered for inclusion in the new gallery.

DISCUSSION QUESTIONS FOR ARTISTIC FACTIONS

Some of the artists and art dealers are classified within specific artistic factions, while others are listed as indeterminate on their individual role sheets. These factions are designed to help players recognize similarities among the paintings and collectively articulate the common characteristics of the following important avant-garde movements of the first half of the twentieth century: cubism, constructivism, surrealism, Mexican muralism, Indigenist art, and abstract expressionism. If your character belongs to one or more of these factions, you may be asked to gather together during today's session. The curators will give you some time to discuss the common characteristics of your paintings among yourselves.

If you are an indeterminate and do not belong to one of these factions, you have two choices. You may place yourself in one or more of these artistic movement/style categories (you must be able to explain why your artwork belongs to or was influenced by a particular movement or style). Or you may opt to remain indeterminate and not join an artistic faction. If you remain independent (or perhaps even form a new faction with other indeterminate players!), you must be able to articulate the reasons behind your decision.

If you belong to an artistic faction, here are some questions to help you and your faction members summarize the main characteristics of your style and explain its significance:

- A variety of major isms emerged during the first half of the twentieth century as part of the European avant-garde. Which of these isms influenced your artwork?
- What specific characteristics of your painting(s) illustrate a connection to your artistic movement?
- How does your painting adapt or modify European artistic styles (e.g., cubism, constructivism, surrealism, or expressionism) to reflect or comment on Latin American realities?
- Using the chronology of artistic movements and styles, pick an artistic movement that came before or after yours. How does your artistic faction differ from this style? Do you share any of the same characteristics?

If you are an indeterminate, think about these questions and talk to other indeterminate players about their ideas to find common ground or perhaps form your own faction.

- What do you think about the term "Latin American art"? Is it too limiting and simplistic as an approach to contemporary art? What other approaches are possible?
- Should the artists selected for the exhibit constitute a diverse representation of gender, race, and ethnicity through their art? Why or why not?
- Do you consider your art political? What are some differences between art that innovates through form/technique and art that depicts politics or a political position through its content?
- How does your art influence the thoughts and actions of its viewers?
- What are the advantages and disadvantages of selecting "art for art's sake"? Should art be selected and enjoyed solely for aesthetic purposes?
- How does your artwork add to an understanding of the different cultures, languages, and peoples in Latin America?

Session 5: What Is Latin American Art?

In today's session we will focus on learning about and understanding the major artistic movements and styles that have defined twentieth-century Latin American art. The art dealers, representing well-known deceased artists from Latin America, will give their formal speeches and provide compelling reasons as to why their client's painting should be included in the gallery. Meanwhile the curators, living artists, and other players will listen closely, ask follow-up questions, and engage the art dealers in conversation about the significance of their selected artwork. Today's session includes an important vote for best speech, which can help one lucky art dealer secure a place for their painting in the new gallery. We will also have time for a lively debate on the topic "What is Latin American art?"

REQUIRED READINGS

Read before coming to class today:

- Chapter 3: The Game ("Major Issues for Debate": "What Is Latin American Art?]; "Basic Outline of the Game": Session 5 ["What Is Latin American Art"])
- Chapter 5: Core Texts (David A. Siqueiros, "A New Direction for the New Generation of American Painters and Sculptors"; André Breton, "Manifesto of Surrealism"; José Carlos Mariátegui, "El indigenismo"; Oswald de Andrade, "Cannibalist Manifesto"; Joaquín Torres García, "A Will to Construct: Constructivist Manifesto"; Diego Rivera, "The Revolutionary Spirit in Modern Art"; Joaquín Torres García, "The New Art of America"; José Sabogal, "In Defense of Indigenist Painting"; "An Interview with Roberto Matta"; and "An Interview with Wifredo Lam")
- Review the museum catalog entries submitted by art dealers only

ASSIGNMENTS DUE

- **Art dealers** will give a formal speech about why their painting should be included in the Prado's new gallery and how their selected work contributes to an understanding of twentieth-century Latin American art. *Note:* The formal speech will be the foundation for a written essay on the artist and how his or her painting is representative of Latin American art, discussing influences, themes, aesthetic style, and historical context. This should be a synthesis of the major issues in relation to the art dealer's artist and artwork. The GM will provide guidance about the length of the speech and how this assignment will be evaluated, as well as the specific due date for the written essay.
- **All living artists, el Duque, and Sr. Lustres** should write down three questions (each one directed to a *different* art dealer): (1) one question should involve the specific "Major Issues for Debate" for today's session ("What Is Latin American Art?"); (2) one question should involve

a core text reading for today; (3) and one question should reference the information provided by the art dealers in their catalog entry. Remember that you can earn blank canvas points for participating actively in today's Q&A session and asking all of your prepared questions.

- **Reminder to living artists:** You are looking for an art dealer to represent you after the Prado competition is over. Listen carefully to the speeches today to decide which art dealers are aligned with your interests (ideological, artistic, cultural) and be sure to ask questions to clarify any doubts. Contracts must be signed by the beginning of Session 7 ("Gallery Decisions").
- **Curators, patron of the arts, and private collector:** Check in with the GM about due dates for your written essay based on the formal speech you gave in a previous session.

ACTIVITIES

- Curators welcome all players back to the Prado and determine the order of the art dealers' formal speeches. After each individual art dealer's speech, allow time for questions by the living artists, el Duque and Sr. Lustres. Each art dealer should be allotted the same amount of time for their speech and Q&A session. Players should be encouraged to ask the art dealers any remaining questions during the open time.
- After all speeches have been delivered, eligible players (i.e., living artists only) vote on the winner of the best speech by an art dealer. The GM will determine when the results are revealed.
- Curators facilitate an open discussion guided by questions on the topic "What is Latin American art?" See suggested topics below.
- Open time for players to network, form alliances, strategize, talk to the curators, ask the art dealers any remaining questions, earn and report blank canvas points, and collaborate with the marketing director.

OPEN DISCUSSION FOLLOWING SPEECHES

The following topics can be used to structure the discussion following the formal speeches by art dealers. The curators can decide which topics or questions will be most helpful in guiding the conversation. Living artists are also expected to have prepared at least one question that directly relates to these prompts.

- **Latin American art and the European avant-garde:** How did the major isms that emerged during the 1920s, 1930s, and 1940s as part of the European avant-garde influence Latin American artists? How did artists from Latin American influence, adapt, and modify European avant-garde styles, including cubism, surrealism, constructivism, and expressionism? Using the core texts, how did Latin American artists understand their relationship to the European avant-garde movements and styles? What are some of the similarities and differences between these artistic movements and styles?
- **The encounter of different worlds:** The colonial legacy of Spain and Portugal forcibly shaped the languages, societal structures, governance, traditions, and religions of Latin America. How does Latin American art represent the history of colonialization by Spain and Portugal? What role does art play in remembering and representing the many and diverse Indigenous cultures that make Latin America unique? How did African cultures influence Latin American art? Why is this important? Who has the right to represent Indigenous or Afro-descendant populations on canvas?
- **National, regional, or international?** Should diversity be defined along geographic and national boundaries to ensure that most, if not all, countries in Latin America are represented in the new gallery? Why is this important? What are some reasons for defining an artist as "international" or "global," as opposed to "Chilean" or "Latin American"? What is your view on cosmopolitanism versus nationalism in the context of

Latin American art? How does a national (e.g., Mexican muralist) or regional (Caribbean painter) identity help a museum audience understand a particular piece of art? What are the advantages and disadvantages of these kinds of classifications for our gallery?

Session 6: Latin American Art and the World Today

In today's session we will hear about some of the exciting new developments in the world of Latin American art. The living artists will give their formal speeches and explain why their artwork should be included in the Prado gallery. The curators, art dealers, and other players will listen closely, ask follow-up questions, and engage the living artists in conversations about the state of Latin American art and the world today. Be prepared for lively discussions about representation, politics, and the future of museums! Today's session also includes another important vote for best speech, which will help one lucky living artist secure a place for their painting in the new gallery.

REQUIRED READINGS

Read before coming to class today:

- Chapter 3: The Game ("Major Issues for Debate": "Latin American Art and the World Today"; "Basic Outline of the Game": Session 6 ["Latin American Art in the World Today"])
- Chapter 5: Core Texts (Gerardo Mosquera, "Good-Bye Identity, Welcome Difference"; Leon Golub, "A Critique of Abstract Expressionism"; Soraida Martinez, "The Art of Verdadism"; Colectivo Situaciones [GAC], "Escraches: 9 Hypotheses for Discussion"; "An Interview with Patricia Rodriguez"; "An Interview with Vik Muniz"; and "An Interview with Fernando Botero")
- Review the museum catalog entries submitted by living artists only

ASSIGNMENTS DUE

- **Living artists** will give a formal speech about why their painting should be included in the Prado's new gallery and how their work contributes to new trends in Latin American art. *Note:* The formal speech will be the foundation for a written essay about the artist and how his or her painting contributes to the world of Latin American art, discussing influences, themes, aesthetic style, and historical context. This should be a synthesis of the major issues in relation to the living artist and their selected artwork. The GM will provide guidance about the length of the speech and how this assignment will be evaluated, as well as the specific due date for the written essay.
- **All art dealers, el Duque, and Sr. Lustres** should write down three questions (each one directed to a *different* living artist): (1) one question should involve the specific "Major Issues for Debate" for today's session ("Latin American Art and the World Today"); (2) one question should involve a core text reading for today; (3) and one question should reference the information provided by the living artists in their catalog entry. Remember that you can earn blank canvas points for participating actively in today's Q&A session and asking all of your prepared questions.
- **Reminder to art dealers:** You are looking for a new artist to represent after the Prado competition is over. Listen carefully to the speeches today to decide which living artists are aligned with your interests (ideological, artistic, cultural) and be sure to ask questions to clarify any doubts. Contracts must be signed by the beginning of Session 7 ("Gallery Decisions").
- **Art dealers:** Check in with the GM about due dates for your written essay based on the formal speech you gave in the previous session.

ACTIVITIES

- Curators welcome all players back to the Prado and determine the order of the living artists' formal speeches. After each artist's speech, allow time for questions by the art dealers, el Duque and Sr. Lustres. Each living artist should be allotted the same amount of time for their speech and Q&A session. Players are encouraged to ask the art dealers any remaining questions during the open time.
- After all speeches have been delivered, eligible players (i.e., art dealers only) vote on the winner of the best speech by a living artist. The GM will announce the winners of best speech by an artist from today's session and best speech by an art dealer from the previous session. The "best speech" winners now have a guaranteed spot in the Prado gallery!
- Curators facilitate an open discussion guided by questions related to the topic of Latin American art and the world today. See suggested topics below.
- Open time for players to network, form alliances, strategize, talk to the curators, ask the living artists any remaining questions, earn and report blank canvas points, and collaborate with the marketing director.

OPEN DISCUSSION FOLLOWING SPEECHES

The following topics can be used to structure the discussion following the formal speeches by living artists. The curators can decide which topics or questions will be most helpful in guiding the conversation. Art dealers are also expected to have prepared at least one question that directly relates to these prompts.

- **Gender and race**: What role do female artists play in the world of Latin American art? Why should this be taken into consideration for the exhibit? What is the racial and ethnic composition of Latin America? How do particular artworks reflect this reality? Should the artists selected for the exhibit embody a diverse representation of gender, race, and ethnicity? Why or why not? How has Latin American art addressed issues of race and gender? Has this changed over time?
- **Art as politics:** How do particular pieces of art add to an understanding of the different cultures, languages, and peoples in Latin America? What are some of the limitations of the label "Latin American art"? How does your artwork address notions of power and representation? What are some differences between art that innovates through form/technique and art that depicts politics or a political position through its content? What are the advantages and disadvantages of selecting "art for art's sake"? Should art be selected and enjoyed solely for aesthetic purposes? Where can contemporary art find a diverse audience? How can a piece of art influence the thoughts and actions of its viewers?
- **The future of museums**: Who will be coming to the Prado to see this exhibit and why? What message does the art send to the viewers? How does this reflect on the Prado's particular history as a purveyor of art in Europe? Are there new modalities of creating, displaying, and viewing art that require museums to adapt their traditional forms of art exhibition and curation? Is the Prado prepared to make these changes?

Session 7: Gallery Decisions

Are you ready? Today is the big reveal! This session is the final opportunity for artists and art dealers who have not yet been selected for the gallery to convince the curators, el Duque, and Sr. Lustres that their work deserves to be included in the new Prado gallery. There are no formal speeches planned, but players are encouraged to take the floor and make their case one last time. Be prepared for passionate speed manifestos, fiery debates, tense negotiations, and true colors to be revealed! Invited VIP guests from the art world may be present to preview the exhibit today. You never know who might be interested in your painting or perhaps have some influence at the Prado, so be sure to talk about the importance of your art and share highlights about the significance of your work in the broader context of Latin American art. This is your last shot!

REQUIRED READINGS

Read before coming to class today:

- Chapter 3: The Game ("Basic Outline of the Game": Session 7 ["Gallery Decisions"]; "Assignments and Templates": "Speed Manifesto"; fig. 5)

ASSIGNMENTS DUE

- **The marketing director** will share a hype/publicity video about the new gallery.
- **Artists and art dealers:** Signed contracts must be submitted to the GM at the beginning of today's session (see Chapter 3: The Game: "Assignments and Templates": "Art Dealer Contract").
- **Artists and art dealers:** You must prepare a speed manifesto (this can be audiovisual, verbal, painted, etc.; YOU ARE ARTISTS . . . BE CREATIVE!) for one last attempt to convince the curators, el Duque, and Sr. Lustres that your artwork should be included in the gallery. If you already have a guaranteed spot in the gallery, your speed manifesto should highlight the merits of your painting and/or your artistic style (see Chapter 3: The Game ["Assignments and Templates": "Speed Manifesto"]).
- **Artists:** Check in with the GM about due dates for your written essay based on the formal speech you gave in the previous session.
- **Sr. Garza** will present the most recent issue of his art journal, *Círculo y Cuadrado*.

ACTIVITIES

- Presentation of the marketing director's hype video, followed by the public reveal of Sr. Garza's *Círculo y Cuadrado* art journal.
- Speed manifestos by artists and art dealers.
- Blank canvas announcement by docent Martín Romero.
- Announcement of vote(s) from el Duque.

- Announcement of vote(s) from Sr. Lustres.
- Final negotiations: During the final negotiations (as the curators talk privately with el Duque, Sr. Lustres, and the marketing director, the remaining art dealers and artists should invite guests to come see their paintings and talk about the merits of their work. You never know when a potential buyer or art patron could show up!
- Art prize announcements.
- Curators announce their final decisions and unveil the final Prado Gallery.

Session 8: Debrief

In this final session, the GM will determine any remaining victory objectives for players and bring the *Prado* game to a close through a debriefing exercise. We will discuss "What really happened?" by comparing our game experience with the historical record, and there will be time to reflect on what you have learned about Latin American art and museum curation. You will be encouraged to exit the game by putting aside your assumed identity, disclosing any remaining secrets or insider information, and providing feedback about your game experience to the GM.

REQUIRED READINGS

Read before coming to class today:

- Chapter 3: The Game ("Basic Outline of the Game": "Game Sessions," Session 8 ["Debrief"])

ASSIGNMENTS DUE

- **All players:** Complete assessment survey (before, during, or immediately after today's session; GM will provide more details)
- **All players:** Find a Latin American art exhibit (online, local museum, catalog), post-2000, and be prepared to discuss in class how it compares to the Prado Gallery's exhibition (*optional*)

ACTIVITIES

The GM will bring the game to a close and lead a debriefing session.

ASSIGNMENTS AND TEMPLATES

Pregame Discussion Questions

Based on the information in Chapter 1 (Introduction) and Chapter 2 (Historical Background), answer the following questions and bring them to "Preparatory Sessions," Session 2 ("Introduction to Latin American Art").

- Who is your favorite painter in the history of art? Why do you like their artwork or style?
- Approximately how many countries make up the region known as Latin America? What languages do they speak in these countries?
- What are some problems that arise when defining Latin American art?
- Read the comments from contemporary Latin American artists in "The Identity of Contemporary Latin American Art" in Chapter 5: Core Texts. Which opinion do you think is the most accurate or important? Why?
- Based on your specific role for the game, which movement or artistic style is the most important? Describe two or three principal characteristics of this movement or style in your own words.

Gallery Walk

Prior to Session 4 ("Gallery Walk"), you should complete a worksheet (fig. 2) for your own painting (artists and art dealers). First, set your painting up, preferably hanging on a wall. Next, stand in front of the painting, about two or three feet away, for four minutes (time it!). This will seem like a very long time, but it will allow your mind to concentrate on the piece of art and notice details that are not immediately apparent by a quick glance. After the four minutes is up, use the assigned readings in the "General Painting and Art Aesthetics" section of Chapter 5 (Core Texts) to complete a close reading of your painting. During Session 4, you will perform a gallery walk for someone else's painting.

Writing Assignments

Each player will have several writing assignments to complete during the course of the game. Due dates are not the same for all players, so pay attention to the assignment deadlines and instructions in your individual role sheet, or to any updated deadlines provided by your instructor. You are responsible for handing in written assignments on the designated due date. In some cases, your instructor may ask you to work on a draft of your written essay during the game and submit the final version after the game has ended. Please remember to ask the GM!

Written Essay

Students should write an argumentative essay based on their formal speech. Due dates and the essay topic will vary according to the different characters' role and may also be modified according to the instructor's guidelines and course objectives. Here are the suggested essay topics:

- Based on your character's definition of "diverse art of Latin America" (using your experience from the game), write an argumentative essay that explains which artworks should be represented in the gallery and why. Include primary source materials and examples from the game. (*Suggested topic for curators and marketing director.*)
- Select two artworks from the game and write an argumentative essay explaining their significance in relation to the history of twentieth- and twenty-first-century Latin American art. Provide evidence to support your case using primary source materials and examples from game. (*Suggested topic for el Duque de Artega, Sr. Lustres, and docent Martín Romero.*)
- Write an argumentative essay, explaining why your painting is significant in the history of Latin American art. Connect your piece to some of the "Major Issues for Debate" in the "What Is Latin American Art?" or "Latin American Art and the World Today" sections. Include at least one reference to the core texts (chapter 5), and refer to

SUBJECT				
What is the main subject of the painting?	*animal*	*human*	*object*	*nature*

Other specific details about this subject?

What is the overall kind of image?	*realistic*	*abstract*	*nonobjective*

What image components do you see?

COLOR

What colors dominate the painting?

Are the dominant colors warm, cool, dull, bright?

What other colors are used in the painting?

First describe your emotional reaction to the color scheme. Then look up the meaning attributed to these colors in "The Dimensions of Color" (chapter 5). What are some similarities and differences?

LINES				
What kinds of lines do you notice?	*straight*	*wavy*	*circular*	*diagonal*

How do these lines direct your eye to read the images?

FIGURE 2 Gallery walk worksheet

FORM AND VOLUME

What geometric forms do you notice?   *circle*   *triangle*   *square*   *diamond*   *rectangle*   *trapezoid*

Are they symmetric? Asymmetric? Solid? Do they have regular or irregular angles and sides?

Do the images appear to take up "real" space, or do they appear flat (two-dimensional)?

PROPORTION

Are the elements in the painting balanced?   *yes*   *no*

Are there particular elements that are exaggerated or that seem unbalanced? Which ones?

CONTEXT

Is there a context that might be relevant to understand this painting?   *historical*   *political*   *religious*   *mythological*

Do you notice any "context" clues in the images?

Scan the painting. Identify the dominant impression you get.

What can the painting as a whole represent?

QUESTIONS

Write two questions that you would like to ask the artist about this painting. You can ask about the formal elements and/or the context.

1.

2.

other paintings in the competition to argue your point. Develop an argument to convince the reader that the painting by your artist should be included in the new Prado gallery, anticipating possible counterarguments and providing specific evidence to support your case. (*Suggested topic for art dealers and artists.*)

Additional Writing Assignments

In addition to the argumentative essay, players will have other opportunities to complete writing assignments during the course of the game. Please refer to individual character role sheets for more details.

- All art dealers and artists must submit an entry to the museum catalog (Session 3 ["Welcome to the Prado"]), following the template in the game book. They may also choose to submit a written piece to *Círculo y Cuadrado* for blank canvas points.
- Curators: Throughout the course of the game, the curators will ask the art dealers and artists about their personal understanding of "Latin American art" and document the responses. This activity is designed to help the curators articulate their own vision for the new gallery. The written answers should be submitted to the GM before Session 7 ("Gallery Decisions").
- Marketing director: Isadora López is responsible for writing the introduction for the exhibition catalog, which will be distributed to all players at the beginning of Session 4 ("Gallery Walk").
- The docent Martín Romero is responsible for assisting the marketing director with the compilation of the exhibition catalog. The docent will gather the individual entries from each artist and art dealers, compile the information, and create a cover for the catalog.
- Sr. Garza plans to revive Joaquín Torres García's journal *Círculo y Cuadrado*, which introduced the avant-garde movements of cubism, constructivism, and neoplasticism to Argentina. Sr. Garza will be actively involved in the recruitment and

editing process of the journal, which will be distributed at the beginning of Session 7 ("Gallery Decisions"). Any players whose work is published will receive blank canvas points.

Catalog Entry

Figure 3 is a template for the catalog entry. The document should fit on a standard 8.5-by-11-inch piece of paper. The marketing director may request a digital copy of the catalog entry. The written entry should be composed of two paragraphs (about 500 words total) that respond to the prompts in the template.

Art Dealer Contract

Figure 4 is a template for the contract between the art dealer and artist. Both parties must agree on the general terms. Conditions can be added by either party (art dealer or artist) for every 10 blank canvas points earned (beyond the basic requirement of 10 points by the end of the gallery walk session). These additional conditions are binding and nonnegotiable. Artists and art dealers sign only one contract. Please ask the GM for additional guidance and refer to the "Contracts for Art Dealers/Living Artists" handout.

Speed Manifesto

An artist/art manifesto can take many different forms and lengths. For the purposes of our competition, we will take the basic elements of a manifesto and condense the presentation to thirty to sixty seconds (maximum). Your speed manifesto can be delivered in an oral, written, or audiovisual format during the gallery decisions session. It should emphasize the most important principles that drive you as an artist or art dealer. Be creative, humorous, provocative, compelling, passionate! This is your last chance to convince the curators, the patron of the arts, and the private collector that your painting or your artist's painting must be selected for the exhibition.

Figure 5 is an example of an art manifesto from the avant-garde period for inspiration. There are also excerpts of a variety of manifestos in the "Movements and Styles" section in Chapter 5: Core Texts.

Insert image of artwork
submitted to the competition

Paragraph 1: Include introductory information (biographical, stylistic, and ideological) about the artist and their painting (in your own words). What makes the artist unique, important, or worthy of being selected for this exhibit? If you are a living artist, use the first person. If you are an art dealer, use the third person.

List actual dimensions
(in meters/cm or feet/inches)

Medium(s)

Paragraph 2: Select one (1) of the discussion questions listed in Session 3 in the game book, and respond from the perspective of the artist or art dealer. Include at least one quote from or reference to a relevant core text.

Year(s) of creation

Name of artist

Country of origin

(Birth year–[death year, if relevant])

FIGURE 3 Catalog entry template

ART DEALER CONTRACT

*This is a contract between _____, an art dealer, and _____,
an artist, made on _____ of the year _____.*

General Terms (*to be negotiated directly by art dealer and artist*):

- This agreement will last a term of _____ month(s) or _____ year(s).

- The art dealer will have the *regional / national / international* rights to the artwork.

- _____ will cover all costs associated with the exhibition of artist's work.

- The art dealer will pay the artist all proceeds due within _____ days of any sale(s).

- In the event of a loss or damage to any artwork from the date received by the art dealer until it is
  returned to the artist, _____ is strictly liable.

- The art dealer is permitted to show the artist's work at: (*circle all that apply*)

  art fairs   public galleries   private showings   art collector events

- In the event that the art dealer does not sell any of the artist's work within _____ *days/months/
  years*, the contract will be terminated.

Conditions (*artists and art dealers can add additional conditions here, one for every 10 blank canvas points
earned, starting with 20 points. In the case of conflicts (e.g., both players earn an increment of 10 points at
the same time but would like to add conflicting conditions), the decision will be made by die roll.*)

1) _____ will have the exclusive rights to Prado Gallery decisions.

2) Upon the sale of any artwork, the art dealer will receive _____% of the sale.

3) _____

4) _____

Signatures of all parties involved:

Artist: Art Dealer:

_____   _____

FIGURE 4 Contract template

MARTIN FIERRO

Periódico quincenal de arte y crítica libre

10 Ctvs.   **10 Ctvs.**

| Segunda época, Año Iº. Núm. 4 | Buenos Aires, Mayo 15 de 1924 | Dirección y Adm.: Bustamante 27 |

MONTEVIDEO SEGUN VARGAS VILA

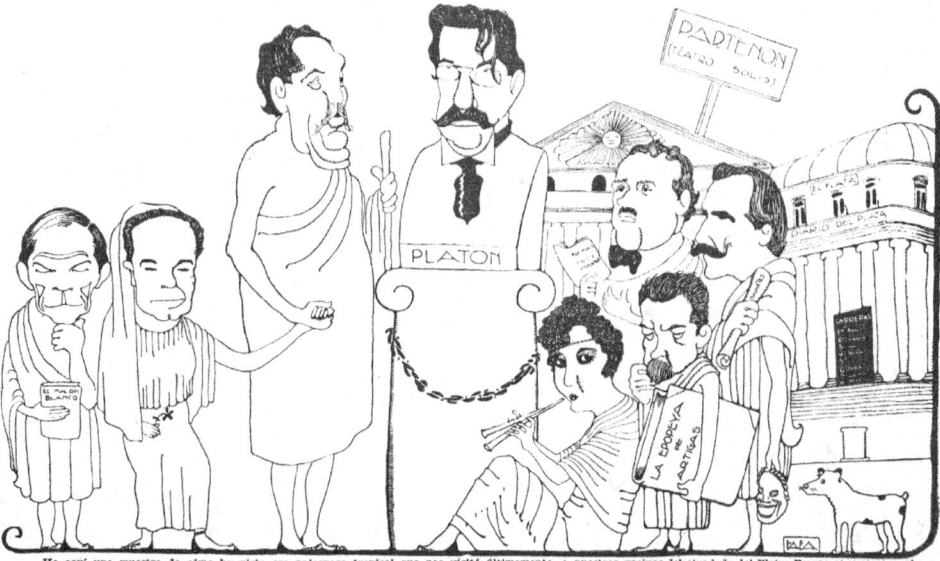

He aquí una muestra de cómo ha visto ese pajarraco tropical que nos visitó últimamente, a nuestros vecinos del otro lado del Plata: Frente al Partenón del Teatro Solís, los griegos del más brillante siglo helénico-uruguayo: Pericles Battle y Ordóñez y Aspasia Brun, que representan la política; la filosofía: Platón-Rodó; las dos máscaras: Sófocles Martínez Cuitiño y Aristófanes Favaro; la elocuencia: Demóstenes Frugoni; la historia: Herodoto de San Martín; la poesía: Safo de Ibarbourou. ¿Y el cuzco de la punta? Pues el perro rabón de Alcibíades, ausente en la vecina calle Yerbal.

Manifiesto de "Martin Fierro"

Frente a la impermeabilidad hipopotámica del "honorable público".

Frente a la funeraria solemnidad del historiador y del catedrático, que momifica cuanto toca.

Frente al recetario que inspira las elucubraciones de nuestros más "bellos" espíritus y a la afición al ANACRONISMO y al MIMETISMO que demuestran.

Frente a la ridícula necesidad de fundamentar nuestro nacionalismo intelectual, hinchando valores falsos que al primer pinchazo se desinflan como chanchitos.

Frente a la incapacidad de contemplar la vida sin escalar las estanterías de las bibliotecas.

Y sobre todo, frente al pavoroso temor de equivocarse que paraliza el mismo ímpetu de la juventud, más anquilosada que cualquier burócrata jubilado:

"MARTIN FIERRO" siente la necesidad imprescindible de definirse y de llamar a cuantos sean capaces de percibir que nos hallamos en presencia de una NUEVA sensibilidad y de una NUEVA comprensión, que, al ponernos de acuerdo con nosotros mismos, nos descubre panoramas insospechados y nuevos medios y formas de expresión.

"MARTIN FIERRO" acepta las consecuencias y las responsabilidades de localizarse, porque sabe que de ello depende su salud. Instruido de sus antecedentes, de su anatomía, del meridiano en que camina: consulta el barómetro, el calendario, antes de salir a la calle a vivirla con sus nervios y con su mentalidad de hoy.

"MARTIN FIERRO" sabe que "todo es nuevo bajo el sol" si todo se mira con unas pupilas actuales y se expresa con un acento contemporáneo.

"MARTIN FIERRO", se encuentra, por eso, más a gusto, en un transatlántico moderno que en un palacio renacentista, y sostiene que un buen Hispano-Suiza es una OBRA DE ARTE muchísimo más perfecta que una silla de manos de la época de Luis XV.

"MARTIN FIERRO" ve una posibilidad arquitectónica en un baúl "Innovation", una lección de síntesis en un "marconigrama", una organización mental en una "rotativa", sin que esto le impida poseer — como las mejores familias — un álbum de retratos, que hojea, de vez en cuando, para descubrirse al través de un antepasado... o reírse de su cuello y de su corbata.

"MARTIN FIERRO" cree en la importancia del aporte intelectual de América, previo tijeretazo a todo cordón umbilical. Acentuar y generalizar, a las demás manifestaciones intelectuales, el movimiento de independencia iniciado, en el idioma, por Rubén Darío, no significa, empero, que habremos de renunciar, ni mucho menos, finjamos desconocer que todas las mañanas nos servimos de un dentífrico sueco, de unas toballas de Francia y de un jabón inglés.

"MARTIN FIERRO", tiene fe en nuestra fonética, en nuestra visión, en nuestros modales, en nuestro oído, en nuestra capacidad digestiva y de asimilación.

"MARTIN FIERRO artista, se refriega los ojos a cada instante para arrancar las tela-

FIGURE 5 "Manifesto de Martín Fierro." Reproduced from the original held by the Department of Special Collections of the Hesburgh Libraries of the University of Notre Dame.

The following is an example of a short but passionate artist manifesto written by David Alfaro Siqueiros in 1922 in his book *Art and Revolution* and signed by all the members of the Syndicate of Technical Workers, Painters and Sculptors, including Diego Rivera and José Clemente Orozco.

A DECLARATION OF SOCIAL, POLITICAL AND AESTHETIC PRINCIPLES

The Syndicate of Technical Workers, Painters and Sculptors directs itself to the native races humiliated for centuries; to the soldiers made into hangmen by their officers; to the workers and peasants scourged by the rich; and to the intellectuals who do not flatter the bourgeoisie.

We side with those who demand the disappearance of an ancient, cruel system in which the farm worker produces food for the loud-mouthed politicians and bosses, while he starves; in which the industrial workers in the factories who weave cloth and by the work of their hands make life comfortable for the pimps and prostitutes, while they crawl and freeze; in which the Indian soldier heroically leaves the land he has tilled and eternally sacrifices his life in a vain attempt to destroy the misery which has lain on his face for centuries.

The noble work of our race, down to its most insignificant spiritual and physical expressions, is native (and essentially Indian) in origin. With their admirable and extraordinary *talent to create beauty, peculiar to themselves, the art of the Mexican people is the most wholesome spiritual expression in the world* and this tradition is our greatest treasure. Great because it belongs collectively to the people and this is why our fundamental aesthetic goal must be to socialize artistic expression and wipe out bourgeois individualism.

We *repudiate* so-called easel painting and every kind of art favoured by ultra-intellectual circles, because it is aristocratic, and we praise monumental art in all its forms, because it is public property.

We *proclaim* that at this time of social change from a decrepit order to a new one, the creators of beauty must use their best efforts to produce ideological works of art for the people; art must no longer be the expression of individual satisfaction which it is today, but should aim to become a fighting, educative art for all.

When writing your own speed manifesto, try to incorporate some of the following characteristics, which are present in many artist manifestos.

- clearly directed to a particular audience (*see first paragraph of manifesto*)
- plural voice ("we") to emphasize collective authorship
- use of strong verbs ("repudiate," "proclaim," "praise") to articulate ideas
- passionate, poetic language ("humiliated," "cruel," "eternally sacrifices")
- strong stance pro/con ("we side with," "decrepit order," "art must no longer be . . .")
- use of italics, bold, different font sizes/styles to call attention to important points or to emphasize certain words

4
Roles and Factions

The Prado Museum Expansion contains historical and living characters from the world of Latin American art. The artists are real people who were living at the time of the game's setting (2010); the art dealers are composite characters who provide an opportunity to bring to life deceased historical artists and their artwork. The Prado Museum staff (curators, marketing director, docent), the patron of the arts, and the private collector were designed, in consultation with a real-life Latin American art curator, to reflect the politics and inner workings behind the creation of a Latin American art exhibition.

Prado museum staff
Sra. Nuria Hernández, curator and expert in twentieth- and twenty-first-century Latin American art
Sr. Roberto Pérez, curator and expert in twentieth-century Latin American art
Sra. Isadora López, marketing director
Sr. Martín Romero, docent

Patron of the arts and private collector
El Duque de Artega, Spanish aristocrat, patron of the arts
Sr. Lustres, private collector of Latin American art

Latin American art dealers
Sra. Amar, expert in Tarsila do Amaral (Brazil)
Sr. Guay, expert in Oswaldo Guayasamín (Ecuador)
Sr. Lomas, expert in Wifredo Lam (Cuba)
Sr. Rivas, expert in Diego Rivera (Mexico)
Sr. Garza, expert in Joaquín Torres García (Uruguay)
Sra. Caló, expert in Frida Kahlo (Mexico)
Sr. Mateos, expert in Roberto Matta (Chile)
Sr. Solanas, expert in Xul Solar (Argentina)
Sra. Varita, expert in Remedios Varo (Mexico/Spain)
Sr. Sabo, expert in José Sabogal (Peru)

Latin American living artists

Eugenia Barrionuevo (Costa Rica)

Fernando Botero (Colombia)

Alonso Delgadillo, "El norteño"
    (Tijuana, Mexico)

GAC (Street Art Group artists collective)
    (Argentina), one to three players

Soraida Martinez (Puerto Rico / New York)

Manuel Mendive (Cuba)

Ruby Aránguiz (Chile)

Joel Corrales Márquez (Cuba)

Yolanda López (Mexican American)

Vik Muniz (Brazil)

BRIEF OUTLINE OF EACH ROLE

The following are listed in alphabetical order by last name.

Sra. Amar, expert in Tarsila do Amaral (Brazil): Sra. Amar represents Tarsila do Amaral, considered one of the leading Latin American modernist artists. Tarsila utilized her own country's Indigenous forms while incorporating the modern styles she had studied—cubism, futurism, and expressionism. Her landscapes include Brazilian vegetation, vivid colors, and geometric, flat shapes with cubist influences.

Ruby Aránguiz (Chile): Ruby Aránguiz is a Chilean artist who believes the visual sensation of her work transcends reality and crosses the bridge into the worlds of poetry and music. Known for her innovative use of light, she has been called a cubist and an impressionist-inspired painter, although her work really defies classification. In many paintings Aránguiz combines the realistic depiction of objects in warm, vivid colors and pale, dreamy backgrounds.

Eugenia Barrionuevo (Costa Rica): Eugenia Barrionuevo did not attend a formal arts school; rather, she is self-taught and has been categorized within the naïve art tradition. She found inspiration in her own multiracial family history, personal experience, and the vibrant Afro-descendant matriarchal culture throughout the Caribbean coast of her home country, Costa Rica. Women, children, family, and neighborhood scenes make up Barrionuevo's regional studies and portraits of Costa Rica's Afro-Caribbean population of Limón.

Fernando Botero (Colombia): As a young artist, Botero traveled to Spain, France, and Italy to study the work of the old masters, as well as Mexico, where he began to explore form. He later began using sculpture to further express volume and mass, expressing that monumentality is a reflection of proportion rather than size. He depicts his figures using flat, bright color and prominently outlined forms, thereby acknowledging the influence of Latin American folk art. While his work includes still lifes and landscapes, he has typically concentrated on situational portraiture.

Sra. Caló, expert in Frida Kahlo (Mexico): Sra. Caló represents Frida Kahlo, a Mexican artist celebrated for her focus on Indigenous culture and female experiences. Kahlo depicted scenes of intense physical and emotional pain that were rooted in her own lived tragedies. Although she has been labeled a surrealist, Kahlo rejected this, saying that she simply painted her own reality. She was married to Diego Rivera, although their relationship was marked by affairs on both sides. In a strange twist of fate, Sra. Caló happens to be the estranged wife of Sr. Rivas, the art dealer for Diego Rivera.

Joel Corrales Márquez (Cuba): Corrales is a young Cuban artist who works within the style of hyperrealism, a technically precise artistic approach to painting that re-creates the look of a photography. Corrales documents the everyday life and people in his home city of Havana, and through his oversized sleeping giants he calls attention to the blind eye society turns to its most vulnerable and marginalized inhabitants.

Alonso Delgadillo, "El norteño" (Tijuana, Mexico): "El norteño" is a muralist who works in and around Tijuana, on the US-Mexico border. His murals portray humanist stories that are surprising and easy to read by individuals who encounter the murals as they walk along the streets on a daily basis. Delgadillo is considered a Mexican neomuralist, indebted to the work of the great Mexican muralists, including Diego Rivera, but far removed from their leftist postrevolutionary ideology.

El Duque de Artega, patron of the arts: El Duque is a wealthy Spanish aristocrat who loves Spanish and European art. He wants to make sure that the selection of paintings in the new gallery at the Prado Museum is of the highest artistic quality. He is wary of highly political art, believing that art should be created for aesthetic purposes. El Duque believes that the new gallery must represent a broad vision of Latin American art, rather than favor one particular country or focus on a small issue within the region.

GAC, Street Art Group (Argentina): Formed in 1997, GAC (Street Art Group) is based on the idea that the artistic and political are part of the same production process. The anonymous members of this group use spaces outside traditional art exhibition venues to confront and single out modes of injustice under democracy. The Street Art Group challenges notions of what it means to be an artist, what art is, and what art's purpose is.

Sr. Garza, expert in Joaquín Torres García (Uruguay): Sr. Garza represents the father of Latin American constructivism, Joaquín Torres García, who spent over forty years of his life in Europe and the United States. Torres García published the journal *Círculo y Cuadrado* (1936–43), and Sr. Garza hopes to revive the publication for a more contemporary readership. Torres García defined his painting as an organized surface structured by the golden ratio rule, in which all of the parts relate to each other and to the whole. Torres García called for artists to change the existing hierarchy of art by valuing Latin American art above European.

Sr. Guay, expert in Oswaldo Guayasamín (Ecuador): Sr. Guay represents the recently deceased painter Oswaldo Guayasamín, considered a national treasure in Ecuador. The eldest of ten siblings, Guayasamín grew up exposed to poverty in the capital city of Quito. His interest in art began at a young age, and in his twenties Guayasamín studied fresco painting under the renowned Mexican muralist José Clemente Orozco. His lifelong work exposed the plight of the downtrodden Indigenous masses, and he is considered the pioneer of "Indigenous expressionism." Guayasamín's images capture the political oppression, racism, poverty, and class division found in much of Latin America. Just like Guayasamín, Sr. Guay strongly believes that art should play a role in advocating for marginalized groups.

Sra. Nuria Hernández, expert in twentieth- and twenty-first-century Latin American art: Nuria Hernández is one of the two lead curators for the new exhibit on Latin American art at the Prado Museum. A native of the cosmopolitan city of Barcelona, Hernández specializes in contemporary Latin American art with a focus on street art, muralism, and the intersections between art and politics. She is very excited to open a new chapter in the museum's history with this groundbreaking exhibit. While the Prado has a long-standing emphasis on the role of Spanish Peninsular art within the international art scene, Hernández would like this new exhibit to reflect some of the ways that Latin American artists have created their own narrative and artistic styles rather than simply imitating or following European artistic movements. She is also interested in learning more about Indigenous representation and influences and showcasing the role of females and female artists in Latin American art.

Sr. Lomas, expert in Wifredo Lam (Cuba):
Sr. Lomas represents Wifredo Lam, an Afro-Cuban painter who was associated with the surrealists. Lam studied the avant-garde in Europe and he also spent time with Picasso, Kahlo, and Rivera before the onset of World War II. Upon returning to his native Cuba, Lam created his own style, fusing surrealism with cubism and reflecting the spirit and forms of the Caribbean in his subject matter. Sr. Lomas is interested in showing how Wifredo Lam was able to make European avant-garde styles his own and bridge the traditions of European art with his unique Afro-Caribbean experience.

Sra. Isadora López, director of marketing:
Isadora López is in charge of communicating with the public all that the new gallery will have to offer. She is very keen on increasing the number of visitors to the Prado, especially in the target demographic range (eighteen to twenty-four years). Sra. López comes to the negotiations with the perspective of the audience, so she would like to see the exhibition contain works of art that she believes new visitors will appreciate. Sra. López will also create a variety of materials for marketing and publicity—she would love your help!

Yolanda López (Chicana): Yolanda López is a Chicana (Mexican American) artist based in southern California, along the US-Mexico border. She created one of her most controversial works in 1978, an updated image of the Virgen de Guadalupe, one of Mexico's most sacred religious and cultural icons, which questions the traditional role of women in Latin American culture. López eschews geographic

boundaries and strongly believes in the power of public art to change negative narratives about Latinos in the United States.

Sr. Lustres, private collector of Latin American art: Sr. Lustres, a private collector based in Spain, is interested in artists who eschew conventional elements of painting in favor of abstract art and political activism. He would like to see art that represents newer trends, and he believes that this would diversify the Prado in a beneficial way. Sr. Lustres is passionate about art that does not shy away from controversial topics, because he sees art as an effective means to communicate important messages to the public.

Soraida Martinez (Puerto Rico / New York):
Born in New York City to Puerto Rican parents, Soraida Martinez is the creator of Verdadism, a form of hard-edged abstract painting accompanied by a written commentary. She is an advocate and humanitarian who bases her art on her life experiences and social observations. She speaks and paints about racism, sexism, and tolerance and believes art can empower people to speak their own truth. Her artwork has been used by educators throughout the United States to teach about diversity and tolerance.

Sr. Mateos, expert in Roberto Matta (Chile):
Sr. Mateos represents Roberto Matta, known simply as Matta, a surrealist painter born in Chile. As a young man, Matta traveled to Europe, where he was invited to join the surrealist movement. He created a distinctive visual vocabulary of biomorphic forms swirling about in eerie settings. Throughout his life, Matta combined the surrealists' interest in psychic automatism with vaguely figural elements caught in states of flux. Upon fleeing Europe during World War II, Matta also became a crucial influence in the development of abstract expressionism in the United States in the 1940s. Indeed, Matta felt very much at home in Europe and later in the United States, building his reputation as a painter mainly outside his native country. His art dealer, Sr. Mateos, is a strong advocate for this kind of cosmopolitan Latin American artist—someone who acknowledges and cele-

brates the influences of Spanish and other European art and artists in their work.

Manuel Mendive (Cuba): Manuel Mendive is an Afro-Cuban artist regarded by many as the most important Cuban artist living today. Clearly influenced by Wifredo Lam and his legacy, Mendive's art is closely intertwined with his African roots and his identity as a santero. Santería is animistic and polytheistic and instills an affinity for nature. In his paintings, Mendive offers a worldview in which humans, animals, and deities exist hand in hand. His work incorporates many different mediums and genres, including drawing, painting, body painting, wood carving, sculpture, and performance that integrates loosely choreographed dance with rhythmic music. Mendive is passionate about recognizing and celebrating the ways that African religion and culture have shaped Cuban national identity and culture.

Vik Muniz (Brazil): Vik Muniz is a Brazilian artist and photographer currently based in New York. Growing up under a military dictatorship, Muniz learned the importance of symbolism and metaphor in the visual arts to circumvent censorship. His work is easily distinguished by the use of unlikely materials, such as dirt, diamonds, sugar, string, chocolate syrup, and garbage, into his photographic process. Influenced by the Brazilian neoconcrete movement, Muniz's work requires an active viewer who is willing to interact with the artwork to create meaning. Muniz's *Pictures of Garbage* series has been met with both commercial success and critical acclaim, and the documentary *Waste Land*, which documents Muniz's creative process, was nominated for an Oscar in 2010. In recognition of his contributions to education and social development, including his work with the *catadores* (garbage collectors) in Río de Janiero's largest garbage dump, Muniz was recently named a UNESCO Goodwill Ambassador.

Sr. Roberto Pérez, expert in twentieth-century European and Latin American art history: Roberto Pérez is one of the lead curators for the new exhibit on Latin American art at the Prado. A native *madrileño*, Sr. Pérez holds a deep appreciation for the long tradition of artistic excellence represented at the Prado. He is a specialist in the European avant-garde, including constructivism, cubism, expressionism, and surrealism and their influence on Latin American art from the early to mid-twentieth century. Sr. Pérez would like to create an exhibit for the Prado that highlights the rich cultural dialogue between Spain and Latin America, regions that are bound together by a shared language, history, and culture. He understands that the artists come from diverse backgrounds and that much of their art is political in nature, but he will be focusing more on technique and style than on ideological messages.

Sr. Rivas, expert in Diego Rivera (Mexico): Sr. Rivas represents the world-renowned Mexican muralist Diego Rivera. Together with David Alfaro Siqueiros and José Clemente Orozco, Rivera was among the leading members of the Mexican muralist movement. Deploying a style informed by such disparate influences as the European avant-garde and Mexico's pre-Columbian heritage, and executed in the technique of Italian fresco painting, Rivera reflected major themes appropriate to the large scale of his chosen art form: first, social and class inequality; and second, the history and fate of Mexico. Due to the space limitations in the new gallery, Sr. Rivas has selected a smaller (but equally stunning) painting to represent his client. On a personal note, Rivera was married to Frida Kahlo, who, interestingly enough, is represented at this competition by Sr. Rivas's ex-wife, Sra. Caló.

Martín Romero: Martín Romero is a college student working at the Prado as a docent, or museum staff assistant. He is at the negotiations to assist the curators, marketing director, art dealers, artists, and patron of the arts. He brings an important perspective as a young adult and member of the target demographic for this new exhibition. Martín is also in charge of the blank canvas points, so all players should report any new activities or points earned directly to him.

Sr. Sabo, expert in José Sabogal (Peru): Sr. Sabo represents the Peruvian painter José Sabogal, who is widely considered the founder of the *indigenista* movement in Peru. Drawing his inspiration from the rural communities in the highlands region of his home country, Sabogal painted majestic and dignified portraits of Indigenous leaders as symbols of a new national identity. Sr. Sabo is an expert in Latin American *indigenista* (as opposed to Indigenous) art, and a passionate supporter of the celebration of Indigenous culture and history through the arts.

Sr. Solanas, expert in Xul Solar (Argentina): Sr. Solanas represents the Argentine painter Oscar Agustín Alejandro Schulz Solari, who changed his name to Xul Solar, meaning "solar light." Xul Solar was an idealist whose translucent and whimsical artwork reflects his utopic vision of a world where everyone spoke a common language. In fact, Sr. Solanas himself is an expert in *neocriollo* (neo-creole), an invented language that Xul Solar created from Spanish, Portuguese, French, English, Greek, and Sanskrit. During his travels in Europe, Xul Solar assimilated the formal techniques of the European avant-garde but deployed these conventions with a highly individualistic style. Sr. Solanas shares Xul Solar's passion for using art to bring people together and believes in the vision of Latin America as a place of harmony and diversity.

Sra. Varita, expert in Remedios Varo (Mexico/Spain): Sra. Varita represents the surrealist painter Remedios Varo, who was born in Spain but frequently moved and eventually settled in Mexico after being arrested during the Nazi occupation of France. Like Remedios Varo, Sra. Varita is the granddaughter of Spanish exiles who fled to Mexico in 1939 during the Spanish Civil War. In Mexico, Varo was inspired by Diego Rivera and Frida Kahlo's work, although she was always viewed as an outsider because of her émigré status. Sra. Varita firmly believes that Remedios Varo (who painted the majority of her pieces in Mexico) embodies a unique cultural blend of Spanish, European, and Mexican influences that speaks to the Prado's theme of the diverse art of Latin America.

FACTIONS

Geographic Factions

For Session 3 ("Welcome to the Prado"), the artists and art dealers should set up their artwork in the following geographic faction groups that represent four regional areas: Andean (Colombia, Ecuador, Peru) and Brazilian artists, Caribbean artists (Costa Rica, Cuba, Puerto Rico), Mexican and Chicano/a artists (Mexico, US-Mexico border, California), and Southern Cone artists (Argentina, Chile, Uruguay). Geographic faction members are encouraged to bring or create national flags to hang near their geographic faction (worth blank canvas points).

Andean and Brazilian artists
  Tarsila do Amaral (Brazil)
  Fernando Botero (Colombia)
  Oswaldo Guayasamín (Ecuador)
  Vik Muniz (Brazil)
  José Sabogal (Peru)

Caribbean artists
  Eugenia Barrionuevo (Costa Rica)
  Joel Corrales Márquez (Cuba)
  Wifredo Lam (Cuba)
  Soraida Martinez (Puerto Rico / New York)
  Manuel Mendive (Cuba)

Mexican and Chicano/a artists
  Alonso Delgadillo, "El norteño"
    (Tijuana, US-Mexico border)
  Frida Kahlo (Mexico)
  Yolanda López (Chicana)
  Diego Rivera (Mexico)
  Remedios Varo (Spain/Mexico)

Southern Cone artists
  Ruby Aránguiz (Chile)
  Roberto Matta (Chile)
  Xul Solar (Argentina)
  GAC, Street Art Group (Argentina)
  Joaquín Torres García (Uruguay)

Artistic Factions

After the gallery walk, artists and art dealers will group themselves according to their specified artistic factions. Some artists and art dealers are listed as indeterminate on their role sheets. In these cases, players may opt to place themselves in one of the following artistic movement/style factions, provided that they can explain *why* their painting was influenced by or reflects a particular movement. If any indeterminate decides to remain independent (or perhaps even form a new faction with other indeterminates!), they must still be able to articulate the characteristics of their artistic style.

Constructivism and cubism
Wifredo Lam (Cuba)
Joaquín Torres García (Uruguay)

Surrealism
Frida Kahlo (Mexico)
Roberto Matta (Chile)
Remedios Varo (Mexico/Spain)

Muralism
Alonso Delgadillo (Tijuana, Mexico)
Diego Rivera (Mexico)

Indigenist art
Oswaldo Guayasamín (Ecuador)
José Sabogal

(Abstract) expressionism
Oswaldo Guayasamín (Ecuador)
Soraida Martinez (Puerto Rico / New York)

Indeterminates
Tarsila do Amaral (Brazil)
Ruby Aránguiz (Chile)
Eugenia Barrionuevo (Costa Rica)
Fernando Botero (Colombia)
Joel Corrales Márquez (Cuba)
GAC, Street Art Group (Argentina)
Yolanda López (US-Mexico border, Chicana)
Manuel Mendive (Cuba)
Vik Muniz (Brazil)
Xul Solar (Argentina)

5
Core Texts

PAINTINGS

Designed as an art competition, the *Prado* game includes visual images, more specifically paintings, as key primary source documents. You should look up the paintings in the competition (see table 4) on your computer to familiarize yourself with the artwork, and the game manager will also make the images available through a learning management system or website. In order to analyze the visual images closely and discuss the artwork critically, you should also refer to the section titled "General Painting and Art Aesthetics" below. Depending on the number of players in the game, the number of paintings may vary. In some instances, additional paintings by these artists will be included in the game.

WRITTEN DOCUMENTS

To play the game well, you must read and have a working understanding of the written documents that follow. When possible, these texts should be referenced by curators, artists, art dealers, and other players in their speeches and debates. The core texts are organized into four sections that serve different functions and align with the game's main learning objectives: formal analysis of art, debates about how to define Latin American art, an introduction to twentieth-century Latin American art movements and styles, and art world and museum dynamics. Although the core texts do not reference every single artist or painting in the game, important ideas about the characteristics of different art styles, the impact of sociopolitical contexts, and the function of art more broadly can be understood through the careful engagement and critical examination of these readings.

TABLE 4 Paintings in the competition

1925	José Sabogal	*La india de Collao*
1927	Xul Solar	*Drago*
1928	Tarsila do Amaral	*Abaporu*
1939	Frida Kahlo	*Las dos Fridas (The Two Fridas)*
1941	Diego Rivera	*El vendedor de alcatraces (Calla Lily Vendor)*
1942	Roberto Matta	*Los desastres del misticismo (The Disasters of Mysticism)*
1943	Wifredo Lam	*La jungla (The Jungle)*
1943	Joaquín Torres García	*Arte universal (Universal Art)*
1962	Remedios Varo	*Vampiros vegetarianos (Vegetarian Vampires)*
1967	Fernando Botero	*La familia presidencial (The Presidential Family)*
1968	Oswaldo Guayasamín	*Las manos de la protesta (Hands of Protest)* from the *Age of Fury* series
1978	Yolanda López	*Portrait of the Artist as the Virgin of Guadalupe*
1990	Eugenia Barrionuevo	*La ventana (The Window)*
1992	Soraida Martinez	*Puerto Rican Stereotype: The Way You See Me without Looking at Me*
2001	Ruby Aránguiz	*Indias caminantes (Walking Indian Girls)*
2007	Manuel Mendive	*Se alimenta mi espíritu (My Soul Is Nourished)*
2008	Vik Muniz	*Nossa Senhora das Graças (Our Lady of Graces)* from the Pictures of Junk series
1999–2010	Grupo de Arte Callejero (GAC)	*Carteles de la memoria (Memory Signs)*
2010	Alonso Delgadillo, "El norteño"	*El bullying (Mural location: Tijuana)*
2010	Joel Corrales Márquez	*El sol para todos por igual (The Sun for Everyone Equally)*

GENERAL PAINTING AND ART AESTHETICS

The following section contains texts that will help you become proficient in identifying the formal elements (subject, form, color, lines, proportion, and context) of a Latin American painting. You should refer to these concepts and definitions often, as you perform close readings of your own painting (as relevant) and other artworks throughout the game. During the gallery walk session, you will learn how to talk (and write) about art using specific, focused language from these texts.

Hermine Feinstein, "How to Read Art for Meaning" (1989)

This guide excerpted from the official journal of the National Art Education Association is designed to help you analyze and understand the formal elements of a piece of visual art. To articulate a compelling and accurate analysis of any painting, the viewer must first understand the basic elements (and meaning) of form, line, proportion, color, subject matter, and context. This guide will be especially useful for the gallery walk session.

Source: Hermine Feinstein, "The Art Response Guide: How to Read Art for Meaning, a Primer for Art Criticism," *Art Education* 3 (1989): 43–53.

To read is to transact with words from a text. The word "text" comes from the Latin *texere*, "to weave or fabricate," something woven together; it commonly refers to literary compositions. Yet much in our environment is fabricated, composed in some way. The visual arts are fabricated and can be read with the same deliberateness required of literary texts. But instead of reading words, words are used to read images. Reading art for meaning implies spending time with it—studying it, rereading it, savoring it. Some knowledge of art vocabulary, art conventions, and art history is required, as well as a framework for deciphering the complex visual array in artworks.

Category I: Description

Description is a general inventory of what you see and what you might know about the work. It involves no interpretations, analyses, evaluations, or preferences. The language used is literal, i.e., factual. It is useful to pretend the work is being described to a blind person.

- Start with the whole, not the parts. What do you see: a painting, sculpture, print?
- Can you guess the approximate size and tell us the spatial orientation?
- What is the overall kind of image: realistic, abstract, nonobjective?
- What image components do you see? In realistic and abstract works, they might be houses, people, animals; in nonobjective works, shapes in both figure and ground.
- Is the overall color warm, cool, dull, or bright? Are the major shapes large or small, curved or angled, vertical, horizontal, or diagonal?
- Provide historical facts, if known: artist's name, title and year of the work, medium used and size of the work, its present location, stylistic label, and attendant ideology that influenced the work.

Category II: Analysis of Form

Now, take a closer look to determine how the work was composed and what materials and techniques were used. This task requires more art vocabulary. It still involves no interpretations, evaluations, or preferences. The gain here is in the further development of visual acuity and language comprehension, both of which are crucial for subsequently constructing metaphoric interpretations. Again, the language used is literal, i.e., factual.

- Identify and analyze relationships among the Principles of Visual Organization: unity, theme, variety, balance, proportion, movement, orientation, placement.

- Identify and analyze ways the Principles of Visual Organization seem to have guided the use of the Elements of Visual Organization: line, shape, form, pattern, texture, space, size, color.
- Identify materials and techniques; analyze their function in the composition.

Category III: Metaphoric Interpretation

What else can the painting's components and the painting taken as a whole represent? What else can it stand for, what else can it mean? Insofar as possible, avoid literal descriptions, analyses, evaluations, and preferences. When interpreting art, one can only infer the artist's intention. The intention, if in fact known, is not to be ignored, but for this particular activity the artist's intention is less important than your interpretation. Metaphor is a process and a product of thought. As process of thought, metaphor organizes, condenses, and vivifies, allowing new insights to emerge and different or deeper levels of meaning to be tapped. As product of thought, metaphor is a nonliteral symbol which can take nonlinguistic or linguistic forms. Art is one such nonlinguistic form. Through metaphor we understand one kind of thing or experience in terms of another of a different kind. Through a painting (one kind of thing) we can understand what joy (another thing of a different kind) can look like. Clustering is an associative search strategy that facilitates metaphoric interpretation. Clustering requires you to quickly spill out intuitive impressions and at the same time to put them into slow motion. It makes impressions visual by capturing them in words in a nonlinear way, allowing you to see your patterns of reactions and generate more.

- Scan the painting. Identify the dominant impression or give the painting a title; note it, circle it, and set it aside.
- Cluster the visual qualities of expressiveness: those of color, e.g., warm, cool, dark, light, dull, bright; those of line, hard, soft, crisp, fuzzy, placement, rough, smooth, big, small, curved, angular, overlapping, empty, horizontal, vertical, diagonal, close, far.
- To those clusters add clusters reflecting your associations generated by the visual qualities.

A few points should be made. First, not all works of art are rich sources for constructing metaphoric meaning. Second, the metaphors you construct may change as you delve deeper into the work and acquire additional knowledge about it; they may change from one viewing to another depending on your mindset at the time. Third, the beauty of metaphoric interpretation is its relative open-endedness. This is to say, it can accommodate multiple meanings provided that they are "referentially adequate."

Glossary of Art Terms

A. IMAGE(S)

In the Fine Arts there are styles of art and kinds of images. Unfortunately, the two are often used interchangeably. Styles of art, such as impressionism, fauvism, surrealism, minimalism, photorealism, refer to historical periods and ideologies. By contrast, images are representations, internally or externally, of something which may or may not be realistic. Distinctions can be made among three general kinds of images (or works of art): realistic, abstract, and nonobjective. The three kinds of images described below do not have rigid boundaries; they are to be thought of as being on a continuum with some overlap.

1. *Realistic Images* refer to commonly understood, nameable objects in the real world.
2. *Abstract Images* also refer to commonly understood, nameable objects in the real world, BUT the images are distorted in terms of form and color and/or are displaced, often with a change of scale. The essence of the Realistic Image, however, is retained.
3. *Nonobjective Images* have minimal referents to nameable objects in the real world, and as such the referents are yet-to-be-named. These images

are of two general kinds: rectilinear (angular) and curvilinear (curved). Nonobjective Images are important [because] they are the structural format of compositions, also known as the picture plane. When one draws or paints, one is obliged to put shapes on a two-dimensional surface, be it paper, canvas, or board. Those surfaces are Nonobjective shapes.

B. PRINCIPLES AND ELEMENTS OF VISUAL ORGANIZATION

The way we organize and process visual information, irrespective of art forms, reflects principles of perception. We see the overall structure. We simplify configurations of forms for ease in recall; attend to affective qualities; see similarities, differences, proximities, continuities, closures. We alternate figure and ground. We see objects in differing degrees of light, distance, and perspective. Many of those principles of perception are reflected in the Principles and Elements of Visual Organization used in the visual arts.

Principles of visual organization:

1. *Unity* is the successful relationship of parts to parts and parts to whole.
2. *Theme* is the dominant and immediately perceptible subject of the work. (Theme usually elicits a literal response and therefore is different from metaphor. Metaphor reflects deeper levels or different kinds of meaning).
3. *Variety* occurs when interest is created through the use of similar, different, or opposing elements. *Note:* Opposition creates tension.
4. *Proportion* refers to quantity, i.e., how much of one thing versus how much of another. Related terms are "dominance/subordinance," "majority/minority."
5. *Balance* is a sense of equilibrium and ranges on a continuum form symmetrical (equal balance) to asymmetrical (unequal balance).
6. *Movement* is a sense of motion created in part by repetition, rhythm, implied line, connect-

edness of shapes and forms, size reduction, tension, overlap, linear perspective, and atmospheric or aerial perspective.

7. *Orientation* refers to the way the entire work is situated in space, i.e., it could be a horizontal or vertical rectangle, a square, or a round or diagonal configuration.
8. *Placement* refers to where in the composition the parts are placed in relation to each other.

Elements of visual organization:

1. *Line* is the path of a moving point in space. A line connected to itself produces a shape. Lines also create edges and boundaries, depict movement, and so on.
2. *Shape* is a two-dimensional configuration which, by definition, possesses height and width. As noted above, a line connected to itself produces a shape. All shapes can be seen as derivatives of one or more of the three basic shapes: the circle, the triangle, and the square.
3. *Form* is a three-dimensional configuration which by definition possesses height, width, and depth. Hence, forms have volume or mass. All forms can be seen as derivatives of one or more of the five basic forms: the sphere, cube, cone, cylinder, and pyramid.
4. *Pattern* is two-dimensional, i.e., flat and consists of three or more units placed at predictable intervals, such as polka dots and stripes.
5. *Texture* is more dimensional than pattern, having highs and lows. Some textures can be felt, others are illusional. A surface can have both texture and pattern, e.g., corduroy.
6. *Space* is itself a shape or form as well as being the picture plane for two-dimensional work, or the space within and surrounding a three-dimensional work.
7. *Size* is self-explanatory; the word "scale" is often used as a synonym.
8. *Color* derives from light, which is energy: no light, no color. Every ray of light coming from the sun is composed of different waves which

vibrate at different speeds. The sensation of color is aroused in the brain by the way the eyes respond to the different wavelengths of light. The brain then interprets those colors as individual stripes in a narrow band known as the spectrum (red, orange, yellow, green, blue, indigo, violet).

Hermine Feinstein, "The Dimensions of Color" (1989)

This section of Feinstein's "Art Response Guide" focuses specifically on the use and meaning of color in painting.

Source: Hermine Feinstein, "The Art Response Guide: How to Read Art for Meaning, a Primer for Art Criticism," *Art Education* 3 (1989): 43–53.

There are three dimensions of color: HUE, VALUE, and INTENSITY. *Hue* is the technical name of a color. *Value* is the amount of light emitted (white being the highest light, black being the lowest; thus, the greatest contrast exists between white and black). *Intensity* is the strength or purity of a color. Adding white to red raises the value of red and lowers its intensity, resulting in pink. Adding black to red lowers the value of red and lowers its intensity, resulting in maroon or burgundy.

Some other facts about color:

a. *Primary colors* are red, yellow, and blue. These are colors which no combination of other colors can produce.
b. *Secondary colors* are orange, green, and violet. These colors, depending on the brand and quality of paint, result from mixing pairs of primaries
c. *Tertiary colors* result from mixing a primary and a secondary color, e.g., yellow + orange = yellow-orange.

d. *Complementary colors* are diametrically opposite on the pigment color wheel (somewhat different complementary colors exist in visual perception and in colored lights). The major pigment complementaries are yellow and violet, orange and blue, red and green. Those colors produce a high contrast similar to that between black and white. And like black and white, when two complementary colors are mixed together in roughly equal proportion, neutralization occurs and a grey is produced.
e. *Warm and cool colors*: Because of their electro-magnetic wavelengths and frequencies, red, orange, and yellow tend to advance, whereas blue, green, and violet tend to recede. However, depending on the sizes and shapes of the surrounding colors, warm colors can be made to recede and cool colors made to advance.
f. *Simultaneous contrast (or after-effects)*: Each color seems to demand its complementary. If the complementary is absent, the eye will produce it simultaneously. For example, a strong green next to a grey will make the grey appear to be red.
g. *Color vibrations* occur when colors are of the same value or intensity are placed adjacent to one another.

Gretchen K. McKay, Nicolas W. Proctor, and Michael A. Marlais, "How to Read a Visual Image" (2018)

This helpful, condensed guide to reading a visual image was adapted from Modernism versus Traditionalism: Art in Paris, 1888–1889. *It should be noted that* Art in Paris *is the first Reacting to the Past game to focus primarily on art history and, more specifically, on the dynamics of the late nineteenth-century Parisian art world.*

Source: Gretchen K. McKay, Nicolas W. Proctor, and Michael A. Marlais, *Modernism versus Traditionalism: Art in Paris, 1888–1889* (Chapel Hill: University of North Carolina Press, 2018), 41–42. Used by permission of the authors.

Style: A style is created when certain formal elements are shared among works of art from a particular time period. So, for instance, there will be some formal similarities for all paintings from surrealism, which is a type of style.

Subject, context: Art always has a subject. You need to be able to discern the subject of your work in order to examine the way the artist goes about painting it. Paintings can also have a context (historical, political, religious, mythological).

Line: Line refers to the type of movement that a painting lends to your eye as you try to look at it. Straight horizontal and vertical lines create an image that is balanced and solid. Diagonal lines in a composition add movement and action. Circular lines move your eye around the composition in a way that is directed by the artist.

Color: The way that color is applied to the canvas affects many things: the way a viewer encounters it, the meaning of the piece, and a viewer's experience of the work. Color can be very bright or more subdued; this refers to its VALUE. Primary colors are blue, yellow, and red. Complementary colors are opposite each other on the color wheel and create a jarring effect when placed next to each other (purple-yellow; orange-blue; red-green). Colors can be of lighter saturation or very highly saturated and bright.

Space, volume: A painting can seem to take up a lot of "real" space, or it can seem flat. If a painting uses perspective (see below), then it will appear to be "real" and create a sense of three-dimensional space. However, a painting is only ever a two-dimensional surface. Artists can "trick" a viewer into seeing three dimensions, but painting, as an art form, is usually on a flat two-dimensional surface. Other artists believe that the ability to show three dimensions on a flat surface is the true mark of an artist: to transform a flat surface into a scene of reality is a wonder and is what makes an artist more than a mere craftsman.

Perspective: To achieve a look of three-dimensionality, an artist often employs one-point linear perspective. In this system, a vanishing point is chosen somewhere on the canvas—in the background. All lines recede back to this one point. These lines that reach back toward the vanishing point are called "orthogonals." Sometimes artists also employ foreshortening to make things that appear in the foreground recede to a sense of "normal" space. Other artists feel that mirroring nature destroys the spirituality of art and thus seek a different way of expressing space and spurn perspective in their paintings.

Proportion: To make a work of art seem true to natural forms, elements should be balanced. This means that, for instance if painting a person, the head and body will be measured in relation to each other. Ideal proportions for the human body change over time in sculpture. In painting, artists can sometimes exaggerate proportions on an individual to make some sort of statement about that person. When an artist does this—deviates from "natural" proportions—he or she does so in order to make a statement. This is an indication that the artist is trying to say something, and it is up to the viewer to attempt to interpret it.

HOW TO DEFINE LATIN AMERICAN ART

The texts in this section are written by Latin American art critics and artists who explore and advance important questions about the identity of Latin American art at different moments throughout the twentieth century. Their ideas engage with a variety of questions from the "Major Issues for Debate" section, including: How did artists from Latin America influence, adapt, and modify European artistic styles such as cubism, surrealism, constructivism, and expressionism? How does Latin American art, in both form and content, reflect or resist the legacy of colonialization by Spain and Portugal? In what ways do artworks reveal the circumstances (Indigenous resistance, colonialization, slavery, immigration, intervention by foreign nations) that have contributed to the complex identity of this region called Latin America? What are some of the limitations of the label "Latin American art"? Who is excluded by this label, and for whom is the term useful? These readings will be especially useful for thinking through the different ways that the term "Latin American art" has been invoked in the past, as well as for articulating how the label can be reimagined in the context of the international art world and museum contexts.

Damián Bayón, "When Will the Art of Latin America Become Latin American Art?" (1976)

In this excerpted article, Damián Bayón (1919–95), a prolific Argentine art critic and journalist who wrote numerous articles about Latin American art, responds to the question of how to define Latin American art. Bayón touches on past concerns such as the influence of European artistic movements and the tendency to classify Latin American art as "exotic" or "folkloric." He rejects the type of "indigenismo fácil" (easy nativism) represented in the work of Peruvian painter José Sabogal. Bayón refuses to characterize "Latin American art" as one particular thing; rather, he celebrates the diversity of styles and voices from the region and artists' ability to create unique pieces that capture a specific cultural moment and that transcend time through formal (technical) innovation.

Source: Damián Bayón, "In Reply to a Question: 'When Will the Art of Latin America Become Latin American Art?,'" *Artes Visuales* 10 [Mexico City, Museo de Arte Moderno, Chapultepec] (April–June 1976): 18–22. Courtesy Carla Stellweg.

I think the art of Latin America will become Latin American art when an artist appears whose sensibility, imagination, and will to synthesize make him capable of achieving an expression that could not have appeared at any other point in time or space. There can be no doubt that a moment arrives in every area of thought, in poetry, in the novel, in music, or in plastic arts, when the attentive and unprejudiced reader or observer says to himself: "This is different!" And I am not speaking here of injecting a few cheap touches of folklore, but rather of acquiring the knack—either purposely or in a sublimely unconscious way of capturing a vital moment in the process of our evolution and giving it a form, a form that sooner or later will become an essential element of the cultural life of a community. And later, to the whole world.

Any number of examples occur to me. I am honest enough, however, to declare at the outset that by this I do not mean resorting to facile "native" touches, as was the case, I feel, with Sabogal in Peru—an academic painter who went to Spain and on returning to his own country set himself, in all good faith, to "translating" Galician farmers and Basque fishermen into Indians of the highlands, without ever having acquired the assurance of the mediocre Spanish painters he imitated. No, I am referring here to what I consider truly authentic Latin America ways of being. Whatever his importance, the Indian will never be a fully representative image of our identity. What is important is not the "figure" that is presented, but what we can say, or want to say, by using that figure (in the broadest sense of the term, since the figure can be an abstract one as in the case of Szyszlo's work, in Peru).

To begin with, and not just because I am writing for a Mexican journal, the name of José Guadalupe Posada seems to me to be one of the most obvious examples to be found in the past century. He has the advantage of having been a naif even before that approach became fashionable. Naif, but at the same time wise in his art, there can be no doubt that Posada's truculence was pure Mexican, and the essence of his times. That is to say, there is nothing more representative of that society and that moment in time than one of his famous skeletons. That is what I call true expression of one's cultural identity, and it seems to me a profoundly Latin American symbol, transcendental rather than superficial. Later came more cultured movements. Mexican muralism was one of them, in spite of its ups and downs.

The examples I have mentioned are "weighty" ones because they are so obvious and indisputable. No less persuasive in the long run, however, are those provided by the isolated efforts of Tarsila do Amaral in Brazil and Torres García, Figari, and Pettoruti in Uruguay and Argentina. They all "raised welts" in their own time: irritating, promoting, stimulating, opening up new roads, forming disciples. And don't come to me with any of that stale gibberish about

Tarsila, Torres García, and Pettoruti having received their formative training in Europe (as did Rivera, for that matter); Orozco and Figari, on the other hand, only went there after becoming fully developed painters.

Personally, it makes no difference to me that Torres García and Pettoruti had links with international movements like cubism, futurism, and constructivism. The truth is that they lived them from within and as protagonists. Why should that be cause today for suspecting artists who, on returning to their respective countries, were to have a lasting influence on the generations that followed them? Do we find cause for reproach in the fact that the Romans went to Greece, or that the Japanese drew inspiration from the Chinese art that was a natural forerunner of their own in history? And in more modern times, does anyone find it strange that Munch and Van Gogh should have gone to Paris to learn all they could from impressionism? Or that Kandinsky, a Russian, adapted first to Munich and then to Paris in the course of his adventures with abstract art? Finally, and almost in our own times, who ever dares to reproach Picasso for not having been sufficiently Spanish? He bore his Spanish heritage within himself, and enriched it during the first forty years of this century in Paris with touches of a French poet and a German-Jewish *marchand*. Nevertheless, the result is the Picasso we know and love.

Where Europeans are concerned, we find no cause for reproaching what we reproach in ourselves, as though we were always obliged to give some special accounting. Why, and to whom? And what is even worse, it isn't outsiders who reproach us, but ourselves, in a pathetic show of cultural masochism. Forgive me, but to me the whole thing smells of reactionary nationalism, or historical revisionism whose goal is to discover whether we are sufficiently Latin American or not.

To me, that is what should be happening in art. Instead of weeping crocodile tears over our hopeless dependence on others and drawing a certain pleasure from the masochism with which we accept our incapability of acting, I think that our first and foremost duty is now, once and for all, to affirm our own personality and take a stand.

The [Latin American] artist—who after all is free to search either within himself or without for inspiration will produce his works as he sees fit. It makes no difference whether they are figurative, neo-figurative, abstract, cinetic, surrealistic, or even conceptual or ecological, or whether they are intended to modify the earth or one's body through the effects of certain techniques involving public videotaped performances. What is essential is that any such manifestation must reveal the imagination and indispensable creativity that enable the artist to produce a specific work that demonstrates some heretofore unknown aspect of his original view of the world.

The time has come, then, to write about them—the plastic artists, that is without falling back on the native touches, folklorism, or local color that so often totally absorb North Americans and Europeans. To us, these artists are not exotic—they are our compatriots, friends or not, but always members of the same spiritual "blood group." Always supposing, that is, that the museums and galleries recognize that all of us—both artists and critics—are acting in good faith, and begin organizing the kind of individual and collective expositions that I have never ceased to demand. ▪

Gerardo Mosquera, "Good-Bye Identity, Welcome Difference: From Latin American Art to Art from Latin America" (1999)

Two decades after Bayón's article, Cuban curator and art critic Gerardo Mosquera proposed a different way of understanding Latin American art in his 1996 essay "Latin American Art Ceases to Be Latin American Art" (1996). In this follow-up article (excerpted), originally published in 1999, Mosquera questions the very term "Latin America," which excludes non-Spanish-/Portuguese-speaking communities, such as Indigenous populations in the region. A key theorist in contemporary debates about Latin American art, Mosquera also rejects rigid geographical boundaries that limit Latin American art, arguing for the inclusion of Chicano/a artists and other Latino/a artists working in the United States. Mosquera calls our attention to the complex circumstances (Indigenous resistance, colonialization, slavery, immigration, intervention by foreign nations) that inform the identity of this region called Latin America. Later, Mosquera notes the tendency to decontextualize Latin American art in the globalized, glossy marketplace, and he cautions against "a simplified notion of art in Latin America," emphasizing instead the diversity of art from Latin America.

Source: Gerardo Mosquera, "Good-Bye Identity, Welcome Difference: From Latin American Art to Art from Latin America" (1999), trans. Michele Faguet, *Third Text* 56 (Autumn 2001): 25–32.

Culture in Latin América has suffered from a neurosis of identity that is not completely cured, and of which this text forms a part, be it in opposition. Within the terrain of the visual arts, this neurosis has manifested symptoms that are particularly acute. Nevertheless, already at the end of the 1970s Federico Morais linked our identity obsession with colonialism, and proposed a "plural, diverse, and multifaceted" idea of the continent, a product of its multiplicity of origin. Yet the very notions of Latin America and Iberoamerica have always been very problematic. Do they include the Dutch and Anglo Caribbean? Chicanos? Do they embrace indigenous peoples who often do not even speak European languages? If we recognize the latter as Latin Americans, why do we not do so with indigenous peoples north of the Rio Grande? ls what we call Latin America part of the West or the non-West? Does this contradict both, emphasizing the schematization of such notions? In any case, today the United States, with more than 30 million inhabitants of "Hispanic" origin, is without doubt one of the most actively Latin American countries. Given the migratory boom and the growth rate of the "Hispanic" population (migration without movement), in a not so distant future, the U.S. may come to have the third largest Spanish-speaking population, after Mexico and Spain. ln some stores in Miami there are signs that say *English Spoken.*

Nevertheless, the idea of Latin America has not yet been discarded, as is the case of the idea of Africa, considered by some African intellectuals to be a colonial invention. The self-consciousness of belonging to a historical-cultural entity misnamed Latin America is maintained, but problematized. The generalized continuance of this recognition may appear strange, since we as Latin Americans have always asked ourselves who we really are. It is difficult to know given the multiplicity of components in our ethno-genesis, the complex processes of creolization and hybridization, and the presence of large groups of indigenous peoples who are excluded or only partially integrated into postcolonial nationalities, and the volume of immigrations and emigrations present throughout the twentieth century. Such an intricate plot is further complicated by a very early colonial history, somewhere between medieval and renaissance, with a permanent and massive settlement from the beginning of Iberians and Africans. There are many answers to the question, maybe already not well outlined, of if we are Western or not, African or not.

Another trap is the assumption that Latin American art is simply derivative of the Western centers, without considering its complicated relationship with modernism and the West.

The new fascination of the centers for alterity, specific to the "global" fad has permitted greater circulation and legitimization of art from the peripheries. But all too often only those works that explicitly manifest difference or satisfy expectations of exoticism are legitimated. As a result, some artists are inclined toward "otherizing" themselves, in a paradox of self-exoticism. The paradox becomes still more apparent if we ask ourselves why the "Other" is always ourselves, never them. Self-exoticism reveals a hegemonic structure, but also the passivity of the artist, of being complacent at all costs. This has been perpetrated, moreover, by local conditions that correspond to an opposition to foreign intrusion. I refer to nationalist mythologies where a traditionalist cult of the "roots" is expressed, supposedly protecting against foreign interferences, and the romantic idealization of conventions about history and the values of the nation. Frequently nationalistic folklorism is to a large extent used or manipulated by power to rhetoricize a so-called integrated, participative nation. In this way the real exclusion of popular strata, especially that of indigenous peoples, is disguised. This situation thus circumscribes art within ghettoized parameters of circulation, publication, and consumption, which immediately limit its possibilities of diffusion and legitimation, reducing it to predetermined fields.

When l said that Latin American art was ceasing to be Latin American art, I was referring to two processes that I currently observe on the continent. One is located in the sphere of artistic production, and the other in that of circulation and reception. On the one hand, there is the internal process of overcoming the neurosis of identity among artists, critics, and curators. This brings with it a tranquility that permits greater interiorization in artistic discourse. On the other hand, Latin American art is beginning to be valued as an art without surnames. Instead of demanding that it declare its identity, art from Latin America is now being recognized more and more as a participant in a general practice that does not by necessity show its context, and that on occasion refers to art itself. This corresponds to the increase of new international circuits that are slowly overcoming the pseudo-internationalism of the *mainstream*. The consolidation of this "third" scene is part and parcel of the processes of globalization. In this way, artists from Latin America, like those of Africa or Southeast Asia, have begun, slowly and yet increasingly, to exhibit, publish, and exercise influence outside of ghettoized circuits. As a result of this, not only are many prejudices confronted and everybody wins, but also those circles with less access to international networks are richly diversified.

However, new problems have emerged. If there exists the danger of self-exoticism in response to the expectation of "primitivism" and difference, there also exists its opposites: abstract cosmopolitanism that flattens out differences, and the mimetic "internationalism" that forces the appropriation of a type of "international postmodern language," much like an English of art that functions like a lingua franca of the increasingly numerous biennales and international exhibitions. The fact that artists from all corners of the globe now exhibit internationally only signifies a quantitative internationalization. The question remains: To what extent are the artists contributing to transformation of the hegemonic and restrictive status quo in favor of true diversification, instead of being managed by it?

The Brazilian modernists used the metaphor of *antropofagia* in order to legitimize their critical, selective, and metabolizing appropriation of European artistic tendencies, a procedure characteristic of postcolonial art. But this process must be qualified to break with connotations that may prove too affirmative, making transparent the battle of who swallows whom, which this relationship implicitly carries. However, the question in its entirety is more complex.

By virtue of the characteristics of an early colonization that Europeanized this vast area, the culture of Latin America, and especially that of the visual arts, has frequently played on the rebound. That is to say, artists have returned the balls that arrived from the North, appropriating hegemonic tendencies and thus turning them into their own individual creativities

within the complexity of their context. Critical discourses have emphasized that such strategies of re-signification, transformation, and syncretism are necessary in order to confront the constant accusation of being copycats and derivatives that, not without reason, we have suffered from. Postmodernity, with its discrediting of originality and its validation of the copy has been of great help to us. But equally plausible would be the displacements of focus that would recognize how Latin American art has enriched the framework of the "international" from within. For example, José Clemente Orozco is always analyzed within the context of Mexican muralism. It would be much more productive to see him as one of the key figures of expressionism, as he is without doubt. Although Wifredo Lam is considered to have introduced specific elements of African origin to surrealism, he has only recently been recognized for having used modernism as a space for the expression of African Caribbean content, thus affirming an anti-hegemonic position.

It is problematic that dominant centers always get the kick-off. One cannot permanently move in the same North–South direction according to the dominant power structure. No matter how valid a different and opposing trans-cultural strategy might be within the dominant structure, it implicates a perennial condition of response that reproduces this hegemony. . . .

When I stated that the best thing that was happening to Latin American art was that it was ceasing to be Latin American art, I was also referring to the problematic totalization that the term carries. Some writers prefer to speak of "art in Latin America" instead of "Latin American art," as a de-emphasizing convention that tries to underline, on the very level of language, its rejection of the suspicious construction of an integral, emblematic Latin America, and beyond this, of any globalizing generalization. To stop being "Latin American art" means to distance oneself from a simplified notion of art in Latin America and to highlight the extraordinary variety of symbolic production on the continent.

Art in Latin America has, since the 1960s, been intermittently displacing the conventional paradigms. These paradigms were related to certain generalizations that are still recognized as characterizations of a slippery Latin American cultural identity, imbedded in magic realism, the marvelous (both related to the surrealist proclamation about Latin America made by André Breton in Mexico), *mestizaje* (miscegenation), the baroque, the constructive impulse, revolutionary discourse, etc. These categories were, however, justified and served the efforts of "resistance" against "imperialist" cultural penetration. They had a notable rise in the 1960s within a militant Latin Americanism characteristic of the historical period marked by the Cuban Revolution and guerrilla movements. However, these ideologies came to over-construct these categories with a totalizing effect, so that they became stereotypes for the outside gaze. To speak today of magic realism or miscegenation as global etiquettes sounds almost like an El Zorro movie. . . .

The term *[Art from Latin America]* emphasizes the active participation of art in "international" circuits and languages. It refers to an intervention that brings with it anti-homogenizing differences and its legitimization within the "international" arena. That is to say, it identifies the construction of the global from the position of difference, underlining the appearance of new cultural subjects in an international arena that until recently was under lock and chain. We cannot say that this arena is now open, but that it does have more doors, and that these can be opened with different kinds of keys. ▪

"The Identity of Contemporary Latin American Art" (2010)

The following excerpts are from interviews with a variety of young Latin American artists who showed their work at the Museo de Arte Contemporáneo de Castilla y León (MUSAC) in 2010. Although none of these artists is competing in the Prado competition, their comments bring to the fore some of the issues that will arise in our game as we explore the complexity of defining Latin American art.

Source: "¿Cuál es la identidad del arte latinoamericano?," *El Cultural*, Sec. Arte (July 9, 2010), www.elespanol.com /el-cultural/arte/20100709/identidad-arte-latinoamericano /2500227_0.html. Translated by Megan Sawicki.

Carlos Amorales (México, D.F. [Mexico City], Mexico)

Due to its geographical complexity, contemporary Latin American art varies depending on the places where it is produced. However, there are common points that make it unique to other areas in the world. Latin America gives the impression of being a failed utopia. Today, in Latin American art, discussions about the recent past, as well as concerns about the social situation, namely the unjust distribution of wealth, are crucial. Curiously, Latin American art has the capacity to digest and use figurative and abstract positions, as well as emotional and conceptual positions. There is a tension between the local and the global that affects all Latin American artists, which implies a constant negotiation between the supposedly "original" cultural codes and those of the public, both local and foreign. Perhaps what defines Latin American art is that ambivalence, that being "in the middle" in a negotiation between different languages.

Tania Bruguera (La Habana [Havana], Cuba)

Latin American art continues to be characterized by a sense of urgency created by certain political and social contexts. Here art is integrated into daily life and enters the world of the real. We can see many cases where art goes out into the streets and is shared with an audience that would not normally go to an art gallery. Latin American art is characterized by the way in which all this is transformed into energy, into intensity. But, more than anything, it is characterized by the inevitable theme of politics. What characterizes Latin American art is, therefore, the way in which it reacts to the time that it must wait to receive the recognition it deserves.

Teresa Margolles (México, D.F. [Mexico City], Mexico)

I do not think there is a Latin American art as such. It would be almost impossible to summarize in a single concept a totality given such different socio-economic realities. The art that is currently produced in Latin America is not defined solely by geography, race, or gender. The forms of production generate different themes, and I think that is their great strength. It is difficult to speak of Mexican art since there are many "Mexicos"—for example, the social situation of the north of the country, whose complexity is absolutely different from that of the south or that of the central region. So the artistic results within a particular country or geographic region respond to many different stimuli, criticism, and contradictions.

Óscar Muñoz (Popayán, Colombia)

The strength and vitality of Latin American art today is a product of its deep relationships with the region and with the diverse processes that are shaped by particular conditions and contradictions. Latin American art has managed to detach itself from idealizations and established stereotypes, both from the outside and from within the territory. Regarding the idea of a Latin American identity, Gerardo Mosquera says it best: "Latin American art today is enjoying one of its best moments, mainly because it is ceasing to be Latin American art."

Carla Zaccagnini (Buenos Aires, Argentina)

One has to ask about the construction of that place, which is not a geographical place, but an ideological construction. I do not think Latin American art has an identity. I believe more in a generational proximity, with artists from inside and outside Latin America. It may be that it has created a series of dialogues, confrontations, and derivations that may end up configuring some kind of historical lineage permeated by geographical issues. ▩

MOVEMENTS AND STYLES

The *Prado* game aims to provide a diachronic introduction to a variety of art movements that have defined twentieth-century Latin American art, including: cubism, constructivism, surrealism, expressionism, Mexican muralism, indigenist art, abstract expressionism, hyperrealism, Chicano art, public/street art, and naïve art. This list is invariably incomplete, as the history of twentieth-century Latin American art is complex and spans a wide range of artists from more than thirty countries. The game offers a window into the diverse styles that have characterized art from Latin America from the early 1900s to the early twenty-first century. The following texts, many of which were penned by leading artists from the region, explore the changing styles, movements and debates that have informed the difficult, perhaps impossible, task of defining Latin American art over the course of a century. As you explore these core texts, refer to the game book's "Major Issues for Debate" section to help guide your reading and understanding of the ideas and concepts developed by the authors.

David A. Siqueiros, "A New Direction for the New Generation of American Painters and Sculptors" (1921)

Originally published in David Siqueiros's magazine Vida Americana: Revista norte centro y sudamericana de vanguardia, *this piece was the earliest avant-garde manifesto by a Mexican artist. Siqueiros, who moved in the same social and artistic circles as Diego Rivera and Frida Kahlo, acknowledges the creative impulse behind European isms (cubism, impressionism, futurism), and clearly appreciates the craftsmanship of master painters who achieved "aesthetic equilibrium" in their work. However, Siqueiros calls on his fellow comrades to look at their own culture and past to construct a new path forward for American art. Here we see the beginnings of the art as politics principles that Diego Rivera asserted over a decade later in his 1932 manifesto "The Revolutionary Spirit in Modern Art." We also glimpse Siqueiros's rejection of an archaeological reconstruction of Indigeneity and his dislike for a nationalist agenda that would limit a more universal understanding of Mexican art.*

Source: David A. Siqueiros, "A New Direction for the New Generation of American Painters and Sculptors" (1921), in *Art and Revolution*, trans. Sylvia Calles (London: Lawrence and Wishart, 1975), 20–23. Reproduced with permission of Lawrence and Wishart Limited through PLSclear.

Our work is mainly extemporaneous, it progresses incoherently and produces next to nothing of permanent worth to match the vigour of our great racial gifts. Isolated from valuable new tendencies against which we reacted with hostility and prejudice, we adopted from Europe only the decadent influences which have poisoned our youth and prevent us from seeing essential values; Spanish art has shown marked decadence from the early nineteenth century; recent exhibitions in Madrid representative of Spanish contemporary art fill one's heart with despair.

Fortunately a new, vigorous group of painters and sculptors, more in tune with the spirit of the times, is emerging in Spain; they are concerned to free themselves from the enormous weight of their traditions and to become more universal; most of them are from Catalonia.

We extend a rational welcome to every source of spiritual *renewal* from Paul Cézanne onwards: the invigorating substance of *impressionism*, purifying *cubism*, in all its ramifications, the *futurism* which liberated new emotive forces (but not that which naïvely tried to annihilate the previous invulnerable process) . . . ; all tributaries of the great river, the many psychic aspects of which we may easily find within ourselves; preparatory theories, generally endowed with fundamental elements which have made painting and sculpture into a plastic art again and enrich it with admirable new factors. We must give back their *lost values* to painting and sculpture, and at the same time endow them with *new values*. We must make our work conform to the inviolable laws of an aesthetic equilibrium as did the classical painters, and become craftsmen as skilled as they; we must regard the ancients as models for their constructed basis and their great sincerity, but we must not use archaic "motifs" which would be exotic for us. *We must live our marvellous dynamic age!* Love the modern machine, dispenser of unexpected plastic emotions, the contemporary aspects of our daily life, our cities in the process of construction, the sober and practical *engineer* of our modern buildings, stripped of architectural complexities (immense towers of steel and cement jammed into the ground); comfortable furniture and utensils (plastic materials of the first order). We must dress our *invulnerable humanity* in modern clothes: "*new subjects*," "new aspects."

We draw silhouettes, filling them with pretty colours; when modelling, we remain engrossed in superficial arabesque and overlook the concept of the great primary masses: the *cubes, cones, spheres, cylinders, pyramids*, which should be the scaffold of all plastic architecture. Let us impose the *constructive spirit* upon the purely decorative; colour and line are

expressive elements of the second rank, the *fundamental* basis of a work of art is the magnificent geometrical structure of *form* and the concept of the interplay of volume and perspective which combine to create depth; "*to create spatial volumes.*"

Artistic theories whose sole aim is to "paint light," i.e. to copy or interpret luminosity ("*luminism*," "*pointillism*" "*divisionism*") are lacking in that creativity which is the objective of art; these are discredited, puerile theories, which we in America have been enthusiastic about for the last few years; they are sick branches of *impressionism*, which *Paul Cézanne* had *pruned* and restored to its essentials: we must make *impressionism* something as solid and durable as the art in the art galleries.

An understanding of the admirable human context of *Negro Art* and *Primitive Art* in general has oriented the plastic arts towards a clarity and depth lost for four centuries in an underbrush of indecision; we must come closer to the work of the ancient settlers of our valleys, the Indian painters and sculptors (*Mayas, Aztecs, Incas*, etc.); our physical proximity to them will help us to absorb the constructive vigour of their work, in which there is evident knowledge of the elements of nature, and these things can be our point of departure. We must adopt their synthetic energy but avoid the lamentable archaeological reconstructions (*Indianism, Primitivism, Americanism*) which are so fashionable today and which are leading us into ephemeral stylisations.

Let us further reject theories postulating a "*national*" art. We must become *universal*; our *racial* and *local* elements will inevitably appear in our work. ▪

André Breton, "Manifesto of Surrealism" (1924)

A variety of artists from Latin America befriended, worked with, or were influenced by André Breton, the French founder of surrealism and author of this manifesto. Heavily influenced by Freud's work on the free association of dreams, Breton stressed the liberation of the imagination and the unconscious mind in the service of creativity and art. For many Latin American artists, the creative process of psychic automatism was the most important part of this movement. This excerpted manifesto outlines the major tenets of surrealism and provides a working definition of the term. During the 1930s Breton traveled to Mexico, and in 1938 he cowrote another manifesto with Diego Rivera and Leon Trotsky titled "Manifesto: Towards a Free Revolutionary Art!" that advocated for total freedom in art, unfettered by political control mechanisms or academic constraints.

Source: André Breton, "Manifesto of Surrealism" (1924), in *Manifestoes of Surrealism*, trans. Richard Seaver and Helen R. Lane (Ann Arbor: University of Michigan Press, 1972), 4–26.

Beloved imagination, what I most like in you is your unsparing quality.

We are still living under the reign of logic: this, of course, is what I have been driving at. But in this day and age logical methods are applicable only to solving problems of secondary interest. The absolute rationalism that is still in vogue allows us to consider only facts relating directly to our experience. Logical ends, on the contrary, escape us. It is pointless to add that experience itself has found itself increasingly circumscribed. It paces back and forth in a cage from which it is more and more difficult to make it emerge. It too leans for support on what is most immediately expedient, and it is protected by the sentinels of common sense. Under the pretense of civilization and progress, we have managed to banish from the mind everything that may rightly or wrongly be termed superstition, or fancy; forbidden is any kind of search for truth which is not in conformance with accepted

practices. It was, apparently, by pure chance that a part of our mental world which we pretended not to be concerned with any longer—and, in my opinion by far the most important part—has been brought back to light. For this we must give thanks to the discoveries of Sigmund Freud. On the basis of these discoveries a current of opinion is finally forming by means of which the human explorer will be able to carry his investigation much further, authorized as he will henceforth be not to confine himself solely to the most summary realities. The imagination is perhaps on the point of reasserting itself, of reclaiming its rights. If the depths of our mind contain within it strange forces capable of augmenting those on the surface, or of waging a victorious battle against them, there is every reason to seize them—first to seize them, then, if need be, to submit them to the control of our reason. The analysts themselves have everything to gain by it. But it is worth noting that no means has been designated a priori for carrying out this undertaking, that until further notice it can be construed to be the province of poets as well as scholars, and that its success is not dependent upon the more or less capricious paths that will be followed.

Freud very rightly brought his critical faculties to bear upon the dream. It is, in fact, inadmissible that this considerable portion of psychic activity (since, at least from man's birth until his death, thought offers no solution of continuity, the sum of the moments of the dream, from the point of view of time, and taking into consideration only the time of pure dreaming, that is the dreams of sleep, is not inferior to the sum of the moments of reality, or, to be more precisely limiting, the moments of waking) has still today been so grossly neglected. I have always been amazed at the way an ordinary observer lends so much more credence and attaches so much more importance to waking events than to those occurring in dreams. It is because man, when he ceases to sleep, is above all the plaything of his memory, and in its normal state memory takes pleasure in weakly retracing for him the circumstances of the dream, in stripping it of any real importance, and in dismissing the only *determinant* from the point where he thinks he has left it a few hours before: this firm hope, this concern. He is under the impression of continuing something that is worthwhile. Thus the dream finds itself reduced to a mere parenthesis, as is the night. And, like the night, dreams generally contribute little to furthering our understanding. This curious state of affairs seems to me to call for certain reflections:

1) Within the limits where they operate (or are thought to operate) dreams give every evidence of being continuous and show signs of organization. Memory alone arrogates to itself the right to excerpt from dreams, to ignore the transitions, and to depict for us rather a series of dreams than the *dream itself*. I would like to sleep, in order to surrender myself to the dreamers, the way I surrender myself to those who read me with eyes wide open; in order to stop imposing, in this realm, the conscious rhythm of my thought.

2) Let me come back again to the waking state. I have no choice but to consider it a phenomenon of interference. Not only does the mind display, in this state, a strange tendency to lose its bearings (as evidenced by the slips and mistakes the secrets of which are just beginning to be revealed to us), but, what is more, it does not appear that, when the mind is functioning normally, it really responds to anything but the suggestions which come to it from the depths of that dark night to which I commend it. However conditioned it may be, its balance is relative. It scarcely dares express itself and, if it does, it confines itself to verifying that such and such an idea, or such and such a woman, has made an impression on it. What impression it would be hard pressed to say, by which it reveals the degree of its subjectivity, and nothing more.

3) The mind of the man who dreams is fully satisfied by what happens to him. The agonizing question of possibility is no longer pertinent. Kill, fly faster, love to your heart's content. And if you should die, are you not certain of reawaking among the dead? Let yourself be carried along, events will not tolerate your interference. You are nameless. The ease of everything is priceless.

4) From the moment when it is subjected to a methodical examination, when, by means yet to be determined, we succeed in recording the contents of dreams in their entirety . . . , when its graph will expand with unparalleled volume and regularity, we may hope that the mysteries which really are not will give way to the great Mystery. I believe in the future resolution of these two states, dream and reality, which are seemingly so contradictory, into a kind of absolute reality, a *surreality*, if one may so speak. It is in quest of this surreality that I am going, certain not to find it but too unmindful of my death not to calculate to some slight degree the joys of its possession.

A story is told according to which Saint-Pol-Roux, in times gone by, used to have a notice posted on the door of his manor house in Camaret, every evening before he went to sleep, which read: THE POET IS WORKING.

Those who might dispute our right to employ the term SURREALISM in the very special sense that we understand it are being extremely dishonest, for there can be no doubt that this word had no currency before we came along. Therefore, I am defining it once and for all:

SURREALISM, *n*. Psychic automatism in its pure state, by which one proposes to express—verbally, by means of the written word, or in any other manner—the actual functioning of thought. Dictated by the thought, in the absence of any control exercised by reason, exempt from any aesthetic or moral concern.

José Carlos Mariátegui, "El indigenismo" (1928)

As a Marxist intellectual and journalist, José Carlos Mariátegui worked to advance the socialist movement in Peru through his journal Amauta *(a Quechua word for teacher or wise man), which boasted a drawing by Peruvian artist José Sabogal on the cover. Founded in 1926,* Amauta *published a series of important debates about the term* indigenismo *and the role of artists in representing the Inca legacy in Peru. Mariátegui was a close friend of José Sabogal, although the latter's paintings of Indigenous subjects, especially from the late 1920s and 1930s, are not regarded as ideologically aligned with Mariátegui's social realist agenda and clear politicization of Indigenous rights. In this excerpted section of a longer essay about contemporary literary (and artistic) trends in Latin America, Mariátegui developed his ideas about the emerging* indigenista *movement in Peru. The essay illustrates the tension between Mariátegui's emphasis on the present conditions of inequality faced by contemporary Indigenous people and the need to redistribute the country's resources to create a fairer system of government and Sabogal's artistic appropriation of the ancestral Indigenous figure as a symbol of national unity. Mariátegui also outlines his understanding of the difference between "Indigenist" and "Indigenous" art and proposes the Inca* ayllu *(commune) system of government as a local model for implementing socialism in Latin America. See also Sabogal's 1943 speech "In Defense of Indigenist Painting."*

Source: José Carlos Mariátegui, "Literature on Trial," in *Seven Interpretive Essays on Peruvian Reality*, trans. Marjory Urquidi (Austin: University of Texas Press, 1971), 268–83. Copyright © University of Texas Press, 1971.

The "indigenous" current typical of the new Peruvian literature is spreading and probably will intensify, but not as a result of the extrinsic or fortuitous circumstances that usually determine a literary fashion. Its significance is more profound. The fact that it coincides and intimately relates with an ideological and social current that daily gathers support among youth is sufficient evidence that literary indigenism reflects a state of mind and of conscience in the new Peru.

The indigenism of our contemporary literature is linked to recent developments. If the indigenous problem is part of politics, economics, and sociology, it cannot be absent from literature and art.

The Indian does not represent solely a type, a theme, a plot, a character; he represents a people, a race, a tradition, a spirit. It is impossible to consider and evaluate him from a purely literary standpoint, as though he were a national color or feature on the same plane as other ethnic elements in Peru.

On closer study, it becomes clear that the indigenist current is not based on simple literary factors, but on complex social and economic factors. Because of the conflict and contrast between his demographic predominance and his social and economic servitude, not just inferiority, the Indian deserves to be the focus of attention in present-day Peru. That 3 to 4 million people of autochthonous race occupy the mental panorama of a country of 5 million should not surprise anyone, especially in a period when this country is trying to find an equilibrium which to date has been denied it by history.

Indigenism in our literature, as may be gathered from my earlier statements, is basically aimed at repairing the injustices done to the Indian. Its role is not the purely sentimental one of, for example, criollo-ism. It would therefore be a mistake to judge indigenism as the equivalent of criollo-ism, which it neither replaces nor supplants.

The Indian is prominent in Peruvian literature and art, not because he is an interesting subject for a novel or a painting, but because the new forces and vital impulses of the nation are directed toward redeeming him. This tendency is more instinctive and biological than intellectual and theoretical. I repeat that the genuine indigenist does not concern himself with the Indian as a source of picturesque character and plot.

A critic could commit no greater injustice than to

condemn indigenist literature for its lack of autochthonous integrity or its use of artificial elements in interpretation and expression. Indigenist literature cannot give us a strictly authentic version of the Indian, for it must idealize and stylize him. Nor can it give us his soul. It is still a mestizo literature and as such is called indigenist rather than indigenous. If an indigenous literature finally appears, it will be when the Indians themselves are able to produce it.

The present indigenist current cannot be equated with the old colonialist current. Colonialism, which reflected the feelings of a feudal class, indulged in nostalgic idealization of the past. Indigenism, on the other hand, has its roots in the present; it finds its inspiration in the protest of millions of men. The vice-royalty was; the Indian is. And whereas getting rid of the remains of colonial feudalism is a basic condition for progress, vindication of the Indian and of his history is inserted into a revolutionary program.

It is clear that we are concerned less with what is dead than with what has survived of the Inca civilization. Peru's past interests us to the extent it can explain Peru's present. Constructive generations think of the past as an origin, never as a program.

The Indian has a social existence that preserves his customs, his understanding of life, his attitude toward the universe. Indian life has a style. Notwithstanding the conquest, the latifundium [large land estate], and the *gamonal* [cacique or hacendado, landowner], the Indian of the sierra still follows his own traditions. The *ayllu* is a social structure deeply rooted in environment and race.

The Indian continues his old rural life. To this day, he keeps his native dress, his customs, and his handicrafts. The indigenous social community has not disappeared under the harshest feudalism . . . even after a long period of collapse, an autochthonous society can rapidly find its own way to modern civilization and translate into its own tongue the lessons of the West. ▪

Oswald de Andrade, "Cannibalist Manifesto" (1928)

In this 1928 manifesto (originally published in Portuguese), Oswald de Andrade refers to the cannibalist (anthropophagic) tendencies of Brazilian modernism, which metaphorically devours other cultures to produce its own unique art. The author was married to artist Tarsila do Amaral, whose painting Abaporu *(1928) takes its title from the Indigenous Tupi Guarani term meaning "cannibal." A sketch of* Abaporu *accompanied the publication of the original Portuguese-language "Manifesto Antropofago." Modernist Brazilian artists celebrated the figurative concept of cannibalism to represent the construction of cultural identity and the battle to liberate themselves from intellectual and artistic dependence on Europe. Written in a playful, free-associative style, the Anthropophagite Manifesto (excerpted here) captures the avant-garde spirit of breaking traditional boundaries.*

Source: Oswald de Andrade, "Anthropophagite Manifesto" (1928), trans. Leslie Bary, *Latin American Literary Review* 19, no. 38 (July–December 1991): 38–47.

Cannibalism alone unites us. Socially. Economically. Philosophically.

The world's single law. Disguised expression of all individualism, of all collectivisms. Of all religions. Of all peace treaties.

Tupi or not tupi, that is the question.

Down with every catechism. And down with the Gracchi's mother.

I am only concerned with what is not mine. Law of Man. Law of the cannibal.

We're tired of all the suspicious Catholic husbands who've been given starring roles. Freud put an end to the mystery of Woman and to other horrors of printed psychology.

What clashed with the truth was clothing, that raincoat placed between the inner and outer worlds. The reaction against the dressed man. American movies will inform us.

Children of the sun, mother of the living. Discovered and loved ferociously with all the hypocrisy of *saudade*, by the immigrants, by slaves and by the *touristes*. In the land of the Great Snake.

It was because we never had grammars, nor collections of old plants. And we never knew what urban, suburban, frontier and continental were. Lazy in the *mapamundi* of Brazil.

A participatory consciousness, a religious rhythmics.

Down with all the importers of canned consciousness. The palpable existence of life. And the prelogical mentality for Mr. Lévy-Bruhl to study.

We want the Carib Revolution. Greater than the French Revolution. The unification of all productive revolts for the progress of humanity. Without us, Europe wouldn't even have its meager Declaration of the Rights of Man.

The Golden Age heralded by America. The Golden Age. And all the girls.

Heritage. Contact with the Carib side of Brazil. *Oú Villeganhon print terre*. Montaigne. Natural man. Rousseau. From the French Revolution to Romanticism, to the Bolshevik Revolution, to the Surrealist Revolution and Keyserling's technicized barbarian. We push onward.

We were never catechized. We live by a somnambulistic law. We made Christ to be born in Bahia. Or in Belém do Pará.

But we never permitted the birth of logic among us.
. . .

The spirit refuses to conceive a spirit without a body. Anthropomorphism. Need for the cannibalistic vaccine. To maintain our equilibrium, against meridian religions. And against outside inquisitions.

We can attend only to the orecular world.

We already had justice, the codification of vengeance. Science, the codification of Magic. Cannibalism. The permanent transformation of the Tabu into a totem.

Down with the reversible world, and against objectified ideas. Cadaverized. The stop of thought that is dynamic. The individual as victim of the system. Source of classical injustices. Of romantic injustices. And the forgetting of inner conquests.

Routes. Routes. Routes. Routes. Routes. Routes. Routes.

The Carib instinct.

Death and life of all hypotheses. From the equation "Self, part of the Cosmos" to the axiom "Cosmos, part of the Self." Subsistence. Experience. Cannibalism.
. . .

We were never catechized. What we really made was Carnaval. The Indian dressed as senator of the Empire. Making believe he's [William] Pitt. Or performing in Alencar's operas, full of worthy Portuguese sentiments.

We already had Communism. We already had Surrealist language. The Golden Age.

Catiti Catiti

Imara Notiá

Notiá Imara

Ipejú.

Magic and life. We had the description and allocation of tangible goods, moral goods, and royal goods. And we knew how to transpose mystery and death with the help of a few grammatical forms.

I asked a man what the Law was. He answered that it was the guarantee of the exercise of possibility. That man was named [Gibberish]. I ate him.
. . .

The determination of progress by catalogues and television sets. Only machinery. And blood transfusers.

Down with the antagonistic sublimations. Brought here in caravels. Down with the truth of missionary peoples, defined by the sagacity of a cannibal, the Viscount of Cairu:—It's a lie told again and again.

But those who came here weren't crusaders. They were fugitives from a civilization we are eating, because we are strong and vindictive like the Jabuti.

If God is the consciousness of the Uncreated Universe, Guaraci is the mother of the living. Jaci is the mother of plants.

We never had speculation. But we had divination. We had Politics, which is the science of distribution. And a social system in harmony with the planet.

The migrations. The flight from tedious states. Against urban scleroses. Against the Conservatories and speculative tedium.

From William James and Voronoff. The transfiguration of the Taboo into a totem. Cannibalism.

The *pater familias* and the creation of the Stork Fable: real ignorance of things + lack of imagination + sense of authority in the face of curious offspring.

One must depart from a profound atheism in order to arrive at the idea of God. But the Carib didn't need to. Because he had Guaraci.

The created object reacts like the Fallen Angels. Next, Moses daydreams. What do we have to do with that?

Before the Portuguese discovered Brazil, Brazil had discovered happiness.

Down with the torch-bearing Indian. The Indian son of Mary, the stepson of Catherine of Medici and the godson of Dom Antonio de Mariz.

. . .

Cannibalism. Absorption of the sacred enemy. To transform him into a totem. The human adventure. The earthly goal. Even so, only the pure elites managed to realize carnal cannibalism, which carries within itself the highest meaning of life and avoids all the ills identified by Freud, catechist ills. What result is not a sublimation of the sexual instinct. It is the thermometric scale of the cannibal instinct. Carnal at first, this instinct becomes elective, and creates friendship. When it is affective, it creates love. When it is speculative, it creates science. It takes detours and moves around. At times it is degraded. Low cannibalism, agglomerated with the sins of catechism— envy, usury, calumny, murder. We are acting against this plague of a supposedly cultured and Christianized peoples. Cannibals.

. . .

Our independence has not yet been proclaimed. An expression typical of Dom João VI: "My son, put this crown on your head, before some adventurer puts it on his!" We expelled the dynasty. We must still expel the Bragantine spirit, the decrees and the snuffbox of Maria da Fonte.

Down with the dressed and oppressive social reality registered by Freud—reality without complexes, without madness, without prostitutions and without penitentiaries, in the matriarchy of Pindorama.

Joaquín Torres García, "A Will to Construct [Constructivist Manifesto]" (1930)

In the first issue (1930) of the French constructivist journal Cercle et Carré, *Belgian poet Michel Seuphor published a lengthy manifesto ("In Defense of an Architecture") enumerating the tenets of the avant-garde constructivist movement in Europe. Uruguayan Catalan artist Joaquín Torres García was a cofounder of the Cercle et Carré group of artists, who were united by their opposition to the dominant surrealist movement in Paris. Constructivism shares a focus on form and abstraction with the earlier cubist movement, but Seuphor and his fellow constructivist artists made a more radical break from the representation of recognizable figures on the canvas. Constructivism responded to the violence and destruction of World War I with a call for order and harmony in art. Complementing Seuphor's titular piece in the first issue of* Cercle et Carré, *Torres García's manifesto, "A Will to Construct" (excerpted here), reveals the artist's dualistic understanding of art and the world (abstract vs. figurative/representational; spiritual vs. material; intellectual vs. sensual; true vs. beautiful). While varied in their individual styles, constructivists were concerned with conveying spiritual transcendence and universal harmony through their abstract paintings. Contrary to Torres García's wishes and knowledge, Michel Seuphor heavily edited the manifesto to highlight his own preference for cerebral, intellectual abstraction over any kind of representation in art. Torres García was hurt by this editorial decision, which caused a rift in their relationship, and several years later Torres García returned to Uruguay and in 1936 began publishing* Círculo y Cuadrado, *the Spanish-language version of this French art magazine.*

Source: Joaquín Torres García, "A Will to Construct" (1930), in *Cercle et Carré and the International Spirit of Abstract Art*, trans. Laura Valeri (Athens: Georgia Museum of Art, 2013), 78–80.

If we have felt the need to come together, it is because disorientation and disorder reign elsewhere. It is to find a basis, to have certainties. And our reason has shown us that this basis is **construction**. In total agreement, we have started out under this banner. What is construction?—From the moment that man abandons direct imitation of nature and makes an image **in his own way**, without accounting for the visual distortion imposed by perspective, that is to say as soon as one draws instead **the idea** of a thing and not the thing in measurable space, a certain construction begins. Furthermore, if one organizes these images, seeking to harmonize them rhythmically so that they relate more to the whole of the painting than to what they aim to express individually, one has already achieved a higher level of construction. But this is not yet construction as we envision it. Before arriving at it, we must still consider the form. As a representation of things, this form does not have a value for itself and one cannot call it plastic. But as soon as this form contains a value **in itself**—that is to say through the abstract expression of its contours and its qualities—it takes on a plastic importance, and it could be said that a work conceived in this way is already akin to a certain construction. One can even go further—to consider the unity of the surface. This surface will be divided, these divisions will delineate spaces, these spaces must **relate to each other**: an equivalence must exist between them so that the unity of the whole remains intact. Putting things in order would already be something, but it is not much. **Creating an order** is what is needed.—We can create order by painting, for example, a naturalist landscape. All painters arrange their canvases more or less in this way. They are in nature as if they are taking a walk. But he who creates an order **establishes a plan**—he moves from the individual to the universal. And there is the importance. Here, it is important to establish something.

Whether there is emotion or reasoning at the root of construction must not matter to us: our only goal is to construct. The opposite of the constructive sense is representation. Imitating something that has already been made is not creating. What good is it to imitate a cavern—is it not better to construct a cathedral! Construction must be, above all, the **creation of an order**.

And, naïvely, all of those who have not studied at the Academy draw in this manner. And that is very good. For, the greater the spirit of synthesis in he who draws, the more he will give us a constructed image. The drawings of Negroes, Aztecs, etc. and the drawings of the Egyptians, Chaldeans, etc. are an excellent example of this. This same spirit of synthesis, in my opinion, is what leads one to realize the construction of the painting as a whole, of the sculpture, and to determine proportions in architecture. And only with this spirit can the work be viewed in **its totality**, in **a single** order, in **unity**. What marvels this rule has achieved throughout the ages! Why has it been neglected? This rule is an anonymous thing, it belongs to no one. The whole world can utilize it **in its own way**, it must be the true path of every honest man. But, if this rule has been commonly used in all ages, what is its modern usage? We have already said it with regard to form: what is useful to us is this absolute value that we give to form independent of what it can represent. And the same is true of structure or construction: it shifts, from simple scaffolding **to order** the forms, to take the place of this scaffolding and constitute the work itself. With that, a duality that has always existed in the painting disappears: the background and the images: when structure takes the place of superimposed images, there will no longer be a duality between the background and the images, and painting will have recovered its original identity: **unity**. ▪

Diego Rivera, "The Revolutionary Spirit in Modern Art" (1932)

One of the tres grandes *(three great) Mexican mural artists, Diego Rivera was a passionate advocate for working-class art that was designed for public consumption and education. In this manifesto, Rivera contrasts his idea of revolutionary public art with the elitist bourgeois concept of "art for art's sake." He touts mural art, with its accessibility and clarity, as an essential tool in the fight for working-class rights. A champion of Indigenous culture in Mexico, Rivera claims that his mural art can be considered a continuation of pre-Columbian art traditions that were suppressed during and after Spanish colonization.*

Source: Diego Rivera, "The Revolutionary Spirit in Modern Art," *Modern Quarterly* 6, no. 3 (Fall 1932): 51–57.

ART is a social creation. It manifests a division in accordance with the division of social classes. There is a bourgeois art, there is a revolutionary art, there is a peasant art, but there is not, properly speaking, a proletarian art. The proletariat produces art of struggle but no class can produce a class art until it has reached the highest point of its development. The bourgeoisie reached its zenith in the French Revolution and thereafter created art expressive of itself. When the proletariat in its turn really begins to produce its art, it will be after the proletarian dictatorship has fulfilled its mission, has liquidated all class differences and produced a classless society. The art of the future, therefore, will not be proletarian but Communist. During the course of its development, however, and even after it has come into power, the proletariat must not refuse to use the best technical devices of bourgeois art, just as it uses bourgeois technical equipment in the form of cannon, machine guns, and steam turbines.

The important fact to note is that the man who is truly a thinker, or the painter who is truly an artist, cannot, at a given historical moment, take any but a position in accordance with the revolutionary development of his own time. The social struggle is the richest, the most intense and the most plastic subject which an artist can choose. Therefore, one who is born to be an artist can certainly not be insensible to such developments. When I say born to be an artist, I refer to the constitution or make-up of his eyes, of his nervous system, of his sensibility, and of his brains. The artist is a direct product of life. He is an apparatus born to be the receptor, the condenser, the transmitter and the reflector of the aspirations, the desires, and the hopes of his age. At times, the artist serves to condense and transmit the desires of millions of proletarians; at times, he serves as the condenser and transmitter only for small strata of the intellectuals or small layers of the bourgeoisie. We can establish it as a basic fact that the importance of an artist can be measured directly by the size of the multitudes whose aspirations and whose life he serves to condense and translate.

The typical theory of nineteenth-century bourgeois esthetic criticism, namely "art for art's sake," is an indirect affirmation of the fact which I have just stressed. According to this theory, the best art is the so-called "art for art's sake," or "pure" art. One of its characteristics is that it can be appreciated only by a very limited number of superior persons. It is implied thereby that only those few superior persons are capable of appreciating that art; and since it is a superior function it necessarily implies the fact that there are very few superior persons in society. This artistic theory which pretends to be a-political has really an enormous political content—the implication of the superiority of the few. Further, this theory serves to discredit the use of art as a revolutionary weapon and serves to affirm that all art which has a theme, a social content, is bad art. It serves, moreover, to limit the possessors of art, to make art into a kind of stock exchange commodity manufactured by the artist, bought and sold on the stock exchange, subject to the speculative rise and fall which any commercialized thing is subject to in stock exchange manipulations. At the same time, this theory creates a legend which envelops art, the legend of its intangible, sacrosanct, and mysterious character which makes art aloof and inaccessible to the masses. European painting throughout the nineteenth century had this general aspect.

At present art has a very definite and important role to play in the class struggle. It is definitely useful to the proletariat. There is great need for artistic expression of the revolutionary movement. Art has the advantage of speaking a language that can easily be understood by the workers and peasants of all lands. A Chinese peasant or worker can understand a revolutionary painting much more readily and easily than he can understand a book written in English. He needs no translator. That is precisely the advantage of revolutionary art. A revolutionary painting takes far less time and it says far more than a lecture does.

Mural art is the most significant art for the proletariat. In Russia mural paintings are projected on the walls of clubs, of union headquarters, and even on the walls of the factories. But Russian workers came to me and declared that in their houses they would prefer having landscapes and still-lives, which would bring them a feeling of restfulness. But the easel picture is an object of luxury, quite beyond the means of the proletariat. I told my fellow artists in Russia that they should sell their paintings to the workers at low prices, give them to them if necessary. After all, the government was supplying the colors, the canvas, and the material necessary for painting, so that artists could have sold their work at low prices. The majority, however, preferred to wait for the annual purchase of paintings made by the Commissariat of Education when pictures were, and still are, bought for five hundred rubles each.

I did not feel that I had the right to insist upon my viewpoint until I had created something of the type of art I was talking about. Therefore, in 1921, . . . I went to Mexico to attempt to create some of the art that I had been exalting. [The regime] gave us walls, and we Mexican artists painted subjects of a revolutionary character. We painted, in fact, what we pleased, even including a certain number of paintings which were certainly communistic in character. Our task was first to develop and remake mural paintings in the direction of the needs of the proletariat, and second to note the effect that such mural painting might have upon the proletarians and peasants in Mexico, so that we could judge whether that form of painting would be an effective instrument of the proletariat in power. But let me note also another fact. In Mexico there existed an old tradition, a popular art tradition much older and much more splendid than even the peasant art of Russia. This art is of a truly magnificent character. The colonial rulers of Mexico, like those of the United States, had despised that ancient [Indigenous] art tradition which existed there, but they failed to destroy it completely. With this art as background, I became the first revolutionary painter in Mexico. The paintings served to attract many young painters, painters who had not yet developed sufficient social consciousness. We formed a painters' union and began to cover the walls of buildings in Mexico with revolutionary art. At the same time we revolutionized the methods of teaching drawing and art to children, with the result that the children of Mexico began producing artistic works in the course of their elementary school development.

To me, art is always alive and vital, as it was in the Middle Ages when a new mural was painted every time a new political or social event required one. Because I conceive of art as a living and not a dead thing.

For the real development on a grand scale of revolutionary art in America, it is necessary to have a situation where all unite in a single party of the proletariat and are in a position to take over the public buildings, the public resources, and the wealth of the country. Only then can there develop a genuine revolutionary art. The fact that the bourgeoisie is in a state of degeneration and depends for its art on the art of Europe indicates that there cannot be a development of genuine American art, except in so far as the proletariat is able to create it. In order to be good art, art in this country must be revolutionary art, art of the proletariat, or it will not be good art at all. ▪

Joaquín Torres García, "The New Art of America" (1942)

After a lengthy stay in Europe, where he attended art schools and frequented the avant-garde scene, Joaquín Torres García returned to Montevideo, Uruguay, and founded a school with the aim of rejuvenating the art scene in his home country. After many years in Madrid and Paris, Torres García was now ready to differentiate himself as a Latin American artist, drawing a clear line between South America and Europe. This essay calls for a unification of artists across the region based on an appreciation of universal geometric forms and "true autochthonous" culture. Pay attention to the tension here between Joaquín Torres García's embrace of the "universal" fundamental principles that can be ascertained from Indigenous monuments, social systems, and cosmology and his dismissiveness of the "contemporary Indian."

Source: Joaquín Torres García, "The New Art of America" (1942), in *Manifestos and Polemics in Latin American Modern Art*, ed. and trans. Patrick Frank (Albuquerque: University of New Mexico Press, 2017), 95–98. Copyright © 2017 University of New Mexico Press.

Today's artists have understood that art cannot be separated from the human problem. Therefore, they should select what each age requires, but only, in my opinion, what it requires in a universal sense; that is, what can unite humans rather than divide them. And in realizing this, art must preserve its purely visual and nondescriptive aspects, because visual creation belongs to a universal order, being based on universal laws. In this way, there is no longer any disparity between the form and what is expressed, for everything joins in perfect unity. Perhaps some artists have misunderstood this urge, in trying to approach human life, because they have believed that the human was only to be found in the anecdotal. But we don't believe that; we have resolved the problem in another way. And by resolving it in this way, we see that we enter fully into the great universal tradition that demands, just as we demand, that both the life and the aspirations of man, along with those of art, should be founded on the pure laws of thought. We establish thereby an objective law that will raise humans above the level of their individuality. This individuality separates humans, while the universal law unites them. Hence, thought of a geometric sort should direct our art and our life.

Across the Americas, a great desire for unification is rising. And although some interpret this urge in a narrow political sense, we ought to contribute to this movement, without losing sight of the primordial, while distancing ourselves from the merely political. We must explore deeper realms, disregarding the purely material aspect and keeping it out of our thoughts.

We are faced with the human problems of all countries, which interest us because they are human in the universal sense. However, without being selfish, we should be even more interested in our own problems. Here we have been given our own ground to cultivate and we must complete our own tasks. For this reason, we already inverted the map, indicating that our North was the South, and so, in a way, breaking our ties to the spiritual tyranny of Europe. Let us reintegrate ourselves, then, into the great Indo-American family.

What we are proposing is not pan-Americanism, but a spiritual union based on a profound relationship that transcends the concept of States. We need an objective toward which to orient our production, and also one to serve as a basis. This would not only define us, in that sense, for ourselves, but also for others. Under the sign of Indo-America, we can march in perfect harmony, basing ourselves on something real, since the artist too must take from the earth. We must be, then, artists of the Americas.

Our generation should be a new one, which attempts to relate to this land by penetrating into its depths. Therefore, we disregard and repudiate the superficial, which, as it has no roots, does not survive here; and this means everything foreign. We must also reject colonialism, the invaders, and the pseudo-culture they created: it is a bitter drink brewed from the worst kinds of alcohol. To be precise, if we want to find stature, nobility, measure, order—that is, what should be called culture—we can find it in the ancient cultures of this continent; there is everything that could elevate, regenerate, and purify us.

Let us build. Form ourselves. Create. A true culture must replace what is commonly called culture here. Not, then, an amalgam of diverse kinds of knowledge and principles, incoherent and random, but something mature and unified: a structure. Something integral, based on a fertile idea, realized in harmonious conjunction.

In recent years, we have already carried out an initial task. The idea of structure, of construction, has been launched, and works have been created in accordance with it. The geometric principle has appeared, and this is already a reintegration into the archaic culture. The idea of the cosmos, of universality, has also been introduced. And, because these ideas did not previously exist among us, we can say that the return to the tradition of the continent begins now—and not through archaeological studies, as in other parts of America, but through the essence of that tradition.

Falling into the archaeological, making South American pastiches, would be an extreme danger that we must avoid at all costs. That is what everyone who has tried to make an autochthonous art has fallen into: Chileans, Mexicans, Peruvians, etc., even including figures such as Diego Rivera. If not that, another stumbling block is just as dangerous: falling into folklorism. For now we seem to have freed ourselves from that pitfall, and I am sure that we will remain free of it. We are equally untouched by the values and qualities of European art that we studied so devotedly. Let Cézanne and Picasso, Matisse and Renoir, remain over there. Let Cubism and Neoplasticism remain over there. And even the masters of all schools. And why not Egypt and Greece, and Byzantium as well . . . because we have here an art as strong and as profound as theirs. It is better for us to study our own, in order to understand its essence.

Let us start from this: We here are not in Western Europe. This is a reality. And although this land was colonized by Europeans, that means nothing; we are

in South America. Their European problem, then, does not have to be our problem. Our culture must have a different origin. This continent is younger; its chronology is not that of the Old World; our prehistory comes later than European prehistory. So the origin of culture here is more recent. Besides, at a certain moment its normal evolution was interrupted by the invaders, which is to say that it was buried for almost four centuries.

The lack of character of these South American peoples is only apparent, for underneath the slight European veneer lies the true autochthonous character. Now what happens is that, due to the European overlay, the true character does not thrive. But with a different consciousness of the situation, it can grow and develop, and this is what should happen. This true character is also threatened by the bastard culture to which I have referred, a sort of covering scar that leaves no outlet for the genuine. One lives in that shadow and ignores a reality whose hour has come. It is time for it to manifest itself. Above all, any exaltation of the invaders and their grotesque manifestations should cease. Because the Indian was a geometer. And that means culture. And through that comes a manifestation of Universal Humanity. With the Indian (and one can hardly speak of the contemporary Indian), we can have a dialogue. His monuments and his cosmic concept of the world, which determined his social system, his calendar, his mythology, and his art: these speak to us eloquently. But such fundamentals, which are similar to those of other lands, here are marked with their own particular structure and qualities. Through them, we must follow the great Tradition of Humanity, but in our own Indo-American way. ▪

José Sabogal, "In Defense of Indigenist Painting" (1943)

José Sabogal gave this speech at a dinner in 1943, shortly after he retired as the director of Peru's National School of Fine Arts. Known as the father of the Indigenist movement in his home country, Sabogal influenced the style of a generation of young Peruvian painters. In this excerpted speech, Sabogal addresses the criticism that was leveled at Indigenist painting and explains his understanding of the controversial and complex term "Indigenist." See also Mariátegui's 1928 essay "El indigenismo."

Source: José Sabogal, "In Defense of Indigenist Painting" (1943), in *Manifestos and Polemics in Latin American Modern Art*, ed. and trans. Patrick Frank (Albuquerque: University of New Mexico Press, 2017), 55–57. Copyright © 2017 University of New Mexico Press.

In 1919, I returned to my homeland after ten years of travel and study in Europe, Africa, and the Americas. I arrived with an exhibition of canvases that I had painted in Cuzco. I did not want to make my debut in Lima with the usual trite scenes of the Seine River, nor with golden impressions of Italy, nor even with the stridently sunny landscapes of Spain or North Africa. My intent was to portray Peru, and, camped out among the primordial walls of old imperial Cuzco, I began a pictorial adventure that later took me all across the country. I hoped through my canvases to reveal hitherto unexpected beauties: the high, snowy peaks and rocky Andean crests, the hushed flat-lands laid out under bulky clouds, the silvery light of the slopes, the shrouded tonalities of the coastal plains, and also the people who inhabited this land of both magic and pain, from the marvelously coppery faces of the Aymara and Quechua peoples, to the yellow-jasmine shades of the Lima women, passing through all the picturesque racial mixtures of our varied land: these were my preferred subjects because they attracted me. And such was my position in the art world, beginning in 1919.

The following year, I was invited to work alongside the founders of the School of Fine Arts. I already grasped the admirable astuteness and judgment of our illustrious [director Daniel] Hernández, who founded the school in that fragile and delicate environment. Upon his death I assumed the difficult job. From the beginning, the public attitude was impatient. Soon, harsh diatribes rang out, sometimes in organized campaigns; but these only swelled the ranks of students who entered our silent and serious halls. We were called "cultivators of ugly art" by those whose tastes ran to pale and washed-out Romanticism. They considered themselves in the right, but their pillowy blows were launched from a belief that has no foundation in the soul of the people, and the people have no use for them. Some of the attackers lacked spiritual foundation as well—which might harmonize better with the people—but they came from the ranks of those we might call "tacky."

Then they labeled us Indigenists, but with malice and surprising ill-will; they accused us of promoting an impossible restoration of Inca ways. But by tarring the Indian races, these upstarts aligned themselves with the Spaniards of the days of the Viceroyalty.

Yes, we are Indigenists, in the true sense of the term; even cultural Indigenists, because we seek our identity in our own soil, our own humanity, and our own times. We do not believe any race to be superior, but we do believe that a new type of person has been born in America. In today's Peru and alongside the group of artists whom I have the honor of defending, we attempt to express that theme, by presenting the genuine physical appearance that defines our nation, just as artists did in ancient times through their own resounding and enduring art.

Our artistic ancestry lies in the era of pitiless aesthetic conflict between the styles of two cultures: Neither the Inca empire nor the empire of the invaders succeeded in dominating Peru. The new humanity that emerged from those two currents first arose in the colonial period, with artistic manifestations that fit neither an Incan nor a Spanish mold, yet with a marked flavor of each. These manifestations of popular art grew up together with the Peruvian identity. They gradually become more defined and resolved, reaching works of high distinction such as the Toritos de Pucará in ceramic, the engraved gourds of the Mantaro region, decorated horse bridles of the northern coast, and the painted altarpieces of Ayacucho: in sum, so many pieces showing simple feeling that speak for a surging popular culture as strong as our ancestors who produced it.

At this memorable event, you who attend honor our work in the difficult but beautiful cause of an art endowed with an identity from our soil. I have felt it appropriate in this aesthetic confession to clear up certain points of confusion and certain twisted interpretations. As in all potent movements, these debates may even be necessary because their heat tempers us.

This, then, is our aesthetic position, which rose up in our country after World War I. Its defining characteristics originated in the complicated times of ancient Tahuantinsuyo, continued during the Spanish invasion, and lasted up to our days. Judging by the size of the audience here present, this view has taken root in the consciousness of a good number of Peruvians.

We should thus undertake, with understanding and sympathy, another stage of evolution, which coincides with yet another world war. Now a new generation of artists has risen up who have done nothing but work with passion and sincerity, and they have added a more modern artistic prestige to the legendary name of Peru.

Leon Golub, "A Critique of Abstract Expressionism" (1955)

The Chilean surrealist artist Roberto Matta was a crucial influence in the early days of abstract expressionism (see interview with Roberto Matta and Peter Busa). Fleeing World War II–era violence and persecution in Europe, Matta befriended many of the younger New York–based artists who were interested in creating new forms of art in the late 1930s and early 1940s. Although the abstract expressionists rejected the formal surrealist approach of examining the mind from a clinical perspective, they did embrace the idea of free play, trusting the paint and the canvas to reveal its own universal meaning. While there is no universal manifesto for the abstract expressionists, this critique by Leon Golub summarizes the main characteristics of the movement and places it within a larger historical context. It should be noted that the eerily realistic photorealism movement which emerged in the 1960s and 1970s is considered in part to be a response to the nonfigurative style of abstract expressionism.

Source: Leon Golub, "A Critique of Abstract Expressionism," *College Art Journal* 2 (1955): 142–47. © 1955 College Art Association, reprinted by permission of Taylor & Francis Ltd, http://www.tandfonline.com on behalf of 1955 College Art Association.

CONTEMPORARY American and European painting has been increasingly identified as abstract expressionist in character. This dominance is apparent in exhibitions and critical literature, particularly in the reportorial journals, *Art Digest* and *Art News*, which attempt to document the art of our times. John Ferren (*Art Digest*, November 15, 1953) states that "abstraction gave us the fresh plastic truths of our time. Abstract expressionism gave a new range to the sensibility involving the whole, 'existential' man. Its humanism is implicit not explicit." Abstract expressionism is an international style, perhaps the most generalized and widespread style that has appeared in this century. To what extent this style approaches anonymity—and paradoxically, in an extremely individualistic era, the intrinsic denial of individuated imagery—must be clarified in regard to the social role of the contemporary artist and any personal transcendence of general form expectations.

The writer would summarize the nature of abstract expressionism as follows:

1. The elimination of specific subject matters and a preference for spontaneous, impulsive qualities of experience.
2. The unfettered brush-discursive, improvisatory techniques-motion, motion organization, and an activised surface.

The artist substitutes for any normative sequence of concepts or experiences an impulse energy dramatized as "instinctual" to a pre-conscious state of mind. Actuality (purpose) is attained by abbreviated means through the "direct" impact of non-referential sensation. "Contact" becomes the meaning. Scratched, scribbled lines or ambiguous forms gesture an ambiguous reality when the artist cannot cope with the contradictory stereotypes of the culture.

The artist seeks an action that is pre-logical, pre-cognitive, and a-moral. Reversion or regression to primitive means, common to the childhood of the race or of childhood itself, can only be a romantic device, as modern man—for all his willful (and perhaps necessary) regressive hopes—must consciously seek and articulate what was once primitively experienced. If this expression cannot be directly achieved and if the sophisticated artist does not reach a residual primacy, his forms only simulate pre-conscious activization.

Especially peculiar to abstract expressionism is the terminological remoteness of the purposes attributed to it. The claims made for one painting could as easily typify works by other artists. James Fitzsimmons characterizes [Georges] Mathieu's painting as a "vast black canvas on which white and scarlet tendrils coil and snap with extraordinary tension. This is the cosmic theater, the universe, the unconscious, the dark night within and around us in which primordial forces are engaged in a life-giving, life-destroying struggle that can only be witnessed at a remove; in dreams, in the photographs of astronomers and physicists and most evocatively, in art." If a critic purports such an explanation, he might well "see" those qualities in a painting. And while that painting might seem to intentionally characterize some such experiences, it might, also, very likely picture none of them, as it is not referential in its reduced state to such meanings in any specific fashion.

The avoidance of content is not uniquely the problem of the abstract expressionist but is inherited from the abstract ideologies of the first decades of this century. Neoplastic or constructivist artists sought (or seek) pure form, a non-idiosyncratic and universal art transcending the discordant images of the time. The abstract expressionists also deny any representative disorder, but their avoidance of the constructivist ideality and the irrational aspect of their "expressionist" bias points up an incapacity to avert some skirmished identification within a crisis situation.

The basic attitudes of abstract expressionism might almost be deduced from its name: expressionism refers as it originally did to violence, subliminal contents—an explosion of self; abstraction indicates general form inquiries, an avoidance of representational imagery and a commitment of visual impulse that is more "classic" or distanced (from any direct introspective impulsion). In a way, abstract expressionism wants a very good thing indeed—the intensity of personal commitment without the specificity such a view ordinarily entails. Gesture! if only to make an anonymous "contact."

The individualism of Renaissance art up through Picasso, Ernst, Miro, etc., has been discarded in abstract expressionism. This is one aspect of the experiential crises of the modern world. Only that rare artist who is iconoclastically remote survives with an intrinsic and personal art. If an art form becomes too "free-floating," that is, disassociated from representative contents, it may lose identification and become somewhat anonymous. Such anonymous objects have been functional in some collective cultures (wherein anonymity was a general social phenomenon integrated in the ways and means of the culture), but are certainly not in evidence in the highly mobile, individualistic Western world—although the aggregates of power (social) and the mechanics of modern society certainly predispose towards anonymous responses.

In such a context, the withdrawal of particular (intrinsic) points of view would emphasize the dangers of anonymous or non-committal attitudes. Abstract expressionism is non-referential and diffuse; for all its practitioners' strenuous efforts, it is deficient in regard to any intense, ideational involvement of the artist. As was stated earlier, the quality of certainty is of such a nature today that the artist is "free-floating" in respect to the contradictory aspects of the culture or in regard to any personal point of view, which can only be achieved through a stringent and introspective demarcation of role. ▪

Soraida Martinez, "The Art of Verdadism" (1999)

In the introduction to her self-titled book, the New York / Puerto Rican artist Soraida Martinez outlines the tenets of the Verdadism style. She positions certain characteristics of her style (such as large areas of flat, primary colors; simple geometric shapes; and abstract figures) as part of the abstract expressionism movement, but notes that Verdadism expands the boundaries of traditional abstract expressionist artwork through its contemporary, multicultural perspective. Indeed, the written commentaries, focusing on sexism, racism, and discrimination, that accompany all of Soraida's paintings are a crucial part of her vision and mission as an artist. Comparing herself to a jazz musician, Soraida has said, "The Verdadist breaks away from following the conventional methods of defining art or the accepted modes of traditional thinking . . . both of which are generally and usually tainted with years of ethnocentrism, cultural biases and racial prejudice." In this text, Soraida focuses on the universality of her message, which is grounded in her specific experience as a first-generation Latina artist living in the United States.

Source: Soraida Martinez, *Soraida's Verdadism: The Intellectual Voice of a Puerto Rican Woman on Canvas. Unique, Controversial Images and Style* (Gibbsboro, NJ: Paint Works Corporate Center, 1999), 3. Reprinted by permission of the author, http://soraida.com.

The art of Verdadism is based on my personal life experiences and my observations on humanity. In this art book, I tell the stories of my struggles . . . including some of my experiences with racism, sexism, and stereotyping. As a woman, I am always striving to make a difference and be heard. Ever since I was a little girl, I have had this intense desire to communicate with the world through my art. My Verdadism is a direct response to the society I live in, which never expected much of me. My hope is that, through my Verdadism art, I can make social change.

It is very important that from the very beginning, I make this crucial point regarding the title of my book: my paintings are about a universal human experience and this book could have just as easily been entitled "The Voice of an Irish or Italian or Jewish Woman." Many individuals of ethnic, racial, and religious backgrounds (both male and female) have told me that they too can relate to the issues that I paint and write about. The Verdadism art herein is a collection of my paintings with social commentaries and the goal is to promote a deeper understanding of the human soul and tolerance.

When I first started my Verdadism art style in 1992, the issues in this book were not openly dealt with. Racism went underground and most people acted as if it did not even exist. Many art establishments even suggested that I leave the social statements out because they thought their viewers did not want to hear about these motifs. I also believe that, due to my subject matter, I was excluded from exhibitions; some institutions even insinuated that my art was risqué. Therefore, it was the colleges, universities, and other education-oriented organizations that were drawn toward exhibiting my Verdadism paintings.

I paint from the perspective of the life experiences of a first-generation New York–born woman of Puerto Rican heritage. My passion for art comes from wanting to speak the truth. Through my Verdadism paintings, I want to be honest with myself, as well as the viewer. It is important that you (the viewer) observe the date that each painting and its accompanying commentary were finished because, in the same way that someone takes a photo of a moment in time, each painting and its accompanying commentary is a snapshot of my thoughts and observations at a particular point in my life.

Since I am documenting my thoughts on personal life experiences and universal human situations, there are still many paintings that I have not yet rendered. I wish to continue doing this throughout my whole life, and in the future, it will be very interesting for me to read some of my own commentaries and find that they no longer are a social problem or that they have already been resolved. As I write this book, some of the issues that I painted about in 1992 are just being addressed.

Through Verdadism, I want to open your mind to new ideas and concepts as well as encourage you to think for yourself. Most people let others think for them and that is why stereotyping exists. It is much easier to think in broad strokes than in fine detail. Through Verdadism, I also want to add a voice that has not been previously heard—in a society that routinely puts people like me into little boxes and literally files them away. This Verdadism art evolved from the point of view of a woman born into an environment and situation in Harlem, New York City, where I could have easily taken a different approach to life. Instead, I chose to turn my life into a positive, caring existence by taking the negativity out of my life and overcoming the many obstacles that were placed before me. Now, I am a painter, a designer and a business owner. The point that I would like to stress is this . . . as long as you put your mind to achieving your goals, you too can achieve whatever you want to accomplish.

Today, I am happy to see that many educators are using my Verdadism art and philosophy to educate students about racism, diversity, and other issues pertaining to humanity. Some of the paintings in this book can also be used to help individuals explore their self-identity. It is my wish that you can enjoy this book, while gaining insight into my thoughts and vision. And I hope that this book can help people everywhere realize that we all share a common human experience in this planet we call earth. As we go into the twenty-first century, I look forward to seeing a more caring, self-actualized society where everyone is treated as an individual and not lumped into groups or labels. ▪

Colectivo Situaciones [GAC], "Escraches: 9 Hypotheses for Discussion" (2000)

Escraches *(acts of public shaming) began in the early 1990s in Argentina and were carried out by the Street Art Group (Grupo de Arte Callejero, GAC) in collaboration with human rights organizations in public protest against the torture and disappearance of dissident citizens by former members of the military dictatorship (1976–83). The act of* escrachar *(slang for "to put into evidence, disclose to the public, or reveal what is hidden") exposed the specific places where the military regime had carried out these acts of injustice with impunity (for example, buildings that were used as detention and torture centers). This excerpt (sections 1, 2, 4, 5, and 6) from GAC's* Escrache *manifesto emphasizes the political nature of public art and positions their work alongside that of revolutionaries such as the Zapatistas in Mexico. The* escraches *are a call to action in the present, establishing a new form of justice for crimes against humanity that have been ignored or disavowed by the state's legal institutions.*

Source: Colectivo Situaciones [GAC], "The Escraches: 9 Hypotheses for Discussion" (2000), in *Genocide in the Neighborhood*, trans. Brian Whitener, Daniel Borzutzky, and Fernando Fuentes (Oakland, CA: Chainlinks, 2009), 43–48.

1

The *escraches* exceed the traditional forms of politics: they are a novel practice that affirms a new sense of politics and of militancy.

In this sense, it's critical to begin to scrutinize it and draw out its implications. Like the Zapatista experience, that of the Brazilian Landless Workers' Movement and many others, the *escrache* creates a new revolutionary subjectivity. To think what the *escrache* signifies and to delineate its actual characteristics is the only way to prevent its interpretation via formulas that today no longer have any currency. This is the objective of this encounter.

2

The *escraches* are, first, a call to struggle, a practical confirmation that transformative action exists now or not at all. They are the opposite of the melancholy of those that wait, seated, for a better world. The *escrache* shows us that struggle doesn't depend on the idea of a glorious tomorrow, on a scientifically demonstrated strategy, nor on a savior who will descend and liberate us.

Because of this, the *escrache* creates a different idea of time, different than that offered to us by capitalism.

For capitalism, the past is already gone, it only exists as passive memory, as *Never Again*. The future is a far-away, vague promise that doesn't depend on us. As such, our present is weak, sad: we are alone, awaiting a miracle.

In the *escrache*, on the contrary, the past acts forcefully; the disappeared live in the present. It is a past that affirms that it is a past of the present. Moreover, the future has already arrived, because it is nothing other than that which we are constructing, that which depends on us: it is the future of the present. Thus, the *escrache* founds a present, decisive and full of potentialities.

The *escrache* is a practice that neither waits nor conforms. It appears today and is for now.

4

The *escrache* creates a different idea and practice of justice, one opposed and antagonistic to formal justice. And with this new justice, it founds a new practice and concept of democracy.

First, "if there is no justice, there is *escrache*." Justice doesn't depend on an institution that embodies it, but on an action that produces it. It is not the institution, the norm, nor even human rights that founds the just, but the act and the concrete practice of justice.

Second, and most importantly, the search for justice does not end with imprisonment nor can it be contained in legal bureaucracies. The struggle expressed by the *escrache* goes beyond the State of Rights and can't be reabsorbed by it. If one, two, or ten of the military genocidists were in prison today, the *escraches* wouldn't cease.

The *escrache* creates a new idea of justice founded in the popular capacity for producing truths that power is not able to neutralize via cooptation. It is in this practice that "the people" becomes an autonomous subject.

5

As a result, the *escrache* functions like a machine. It does not matter how many people participate in it, nor how it was organized. When it begins to act, it works with an infectious radicality: it shakes up the neighborhood and spontaneously incorporates people.

6

The contribution and importance of the *escrache* is singular, specific. It is the search for justice and nothing more. It is because of this (and not in spite of it) that it is so powerful. Because of this it also universal; and it is via this singularity that we feel a part of it and we feel expressed within it.

The *escrache* shows us that the vanguards of today are defined by their concrete practices and not by their opinions. And it also shows that all political practice, be it vanguard, alternative, or revolutionary, is singular and situated.

INTERVIEWS WITH ARTISTS

Hearing the voices of the artists themselves offers a unique glimpse into the influences and inspirations that have contributed to the creation of powerful pieces of art—artworks that have stood the test of time. These interviews with Chilean painter Roberto Matta, Chicana muralist Patricia Rodriguez, Afro-Cuban painter Wifredo Lam, Ecuadorian painter Oswaldo Guayasamín, Brazilian mixed-media artist Vik Muniz, and Colombian artist and sculptor Fernando Botero provide an array of opinions and perspectives directly from Latin American artists who are represented in the game. Living artists and art dealers are encouraged to incorporate direct quotes from these interviews in their speeches and debates to help bring to life the voices and concerns of influential Latin American artists.

An Interview with Roberto Matta (1967)

This excerpted interview with Roberto Matta and Peter Busa (a close colleague of Jackson Pollock and an important figure in abstract expressionism) was conducted by Sidney Simon, who published it in Art International *to provide insight into the early days of the New York School's study sessions. The abstract expressionists rejected the Dali-esque concept of surrealism as the visual illustration of dreams, in which archetypal images and figures were depicted in a realistic style. However, they did adopt the role of the unconscious and the freedom of the creative process largely through Matta's influence. As Busa notes: "It was your presence, Matta, that personalized Surrealism for us" (17). This wide-ranging conversation touches on Matta's interactions with the artists from the New York School from his arrival to the United States in 1939 until roughly 1943. Matta was a mentor figure to these artists, although he never fully embraced the need to create purely abstract representations on the canvas and his paintings were not, therefore, considered part of abstract expressionism. The hyperrealism movement arose later partly as a rejection of this kind of abstract painting that was perceived as elitist and distant.*

Source: Sidney Simon, "Concerning the Beginnings of the New York School, 1939–1943: An Interview with Peter Busa and Matta," *Art International* (Summer 1967): 17–20.

SIMON: Your exile from Europe began when, Matta?

MATTA: In October 1939. I had already joined the Surrealist group. I had signed too many anti-Hitler and anti-Stalin papers not to be persecuted by the SS.

SIMON: Tell me something about your life in New York.

MATTA: In New York, I lived rather poorly at first. I found an apartment at 15 Gay Street, near 8th Street and 6th Avenue. It was there that I began to paint and to meet the younger American artists. . . . The New York situation was very strange to me. There were—how would I say it?—many artists who knew something about European art. But it was as if "art" was something not *in Europe* but something *imported to America*. Do you know what I mean? Art was something rare and artificial instead of being an expression of a man.

BUSA: [Matta] was the first big influence on a small group of us. The wonderful thing about Matta's stimulus was his grasp of the morphology of paint. From him we got the idea that paint could transcend the fact that it was just something on the canvas.

SIMON: I'm not sure I get exactly what it is you're saying.

BUSA: Paint was not just paint; it could become crushed jewels, air, even laughter. It was quite open. It had that tremendous possibility of transformation, which we hadn't recognized before. And we wouldn't have recognized it had it not been for the stimulation we got from each other.

MATTA: These artists I started meeting—yourself, [Jackson] Pollock, [Gerome] Kamrowski, [William] Baziotes, [Robert] Motherwell—were full of vitality. But in some funny way they were painting from color reproductions instead of painting about themselves. You know what I mean? Actually they had a fantastic experience to report—the experience of America. To me, this was fascinating. And this automatic technique of the Surrealists (which means to show the functioning of the mind) fit them like a glove. They were very professional. They knew a great deal! As a matter of fact, they knew even more than we Surrealists knew about art history.

BUSA: But to know *history* gave the American artist a greater chance to reject *history*. Look at what happened. We had to start somewhere. We had this healthy attitude of anti-art which for many of us became personalized as self-destruction. The point I am making is this: we were, all of us, really abstract painters, so that our idea of this role of the imagination differed greatly from Surrealism. It was a fuse which lit up the American scene. But from where? It was *your* presence, Matta, that personalized Surrealism for us. But to get back to the popular notion of Surrealism as we understood it. We knew about Dali. We knew that Dali was a kind of illustrator. The dirtiest word you could call an artist then was an "illustrator." We considered Dali as an illustrator of dreams, an artist without plastic consciousness. That is why most of us dismissed Dali as an influence. . . . What I was getting at was our antagonism to Surrealism. Don't you remember how it was expressed even in our discussions in the group? I remember that quite well. That's why I asked you the other day if you still consider yourself a Surrealist. Because though you were one of the Surrealists, you were *something new*.

MATTA: I always defended Breton's definition of Surrealism, which has to do with the total emancipation of man. Surrealism is "more reality." There is always the need for man to grasp "more reality"; for only in this way can we create a truly *human* condition.

SIMON: When did the issue of "scale" enter into your thinking?

BUSA: Almost immediately after our contact with Matta. American artists hardly ever attempted large canvases. We always had this idea that we were making pictures instead of the pictures making us. The change in our thinking stemmed from a sense of relief which resulted from a feeling that we were breaking down the barriers between art and life. This feeling freed our sense of scale.

SIMON: Do I understand you to mean that it was Matta who inspired you in this direction?

BUSA: Yes, very profoundly. Matta's idea was that we have a rich world within and don't have to look for it outside ourselves. It was an idea that combined, ultimately, brilliance of the mind with enthusiasm of the act.

MATTA: To me the *image* always represented an *act*. The action of the imagination is somehow more valid to me, more developed, than the action of the arm. ▨

An Interview with Patricia Rodriguez (1977)

Patricia Rodriguez was one of the founding members of the Mujeres Muralistas (Muralist Women). This interview took place in the late 1970s, and Rodriguez notes the lack of recognition for Chicano art at the time. She also emphasizes the importance of collectivity and sacrifice in the face of struggle—core values not only for the Mujeres Muralistas but also for the wider Chicano movement, which fought for autonomy for Mexican American communities in the United States during the 1970s.

Source: "Mujeres Muralistas: Interview with Patricia Rodríguez," in *The Fifth Sun: Contemporary/Traditional Chicano and Latino Art* (Berkeley, CA: University Art Museum, 1977), 14–15.

Q. Mujeres Muralistas was formed in 1973. Since that time what have been the most important experiences the group has had?

A. Well, we've had a lot of publicity. People admire us for what we are as a group and as women. We always get compliments from other Chicanas; they tell us that we have lots of courage.

Courage is one thing, but being persistent is just as important. When you persist in going to school, or when you work hard as something, you become better at it, no matter what it is. We persisted once we realized that murals are important, and that people really like them. We have enjoyed doing our murals. We have pioneered, initiated something that had not been done before. In other words, a group of Chicanas actually put up scaffolding as men do; we have actually done the painting, and we have enjoyed it all thoroughly. Our persistence in making murals has made us better painters and better artists because we have worked as a group.

Consuelo Mendez, Irene Pérez, Graciela Carillo and I were the four original Mujeres Muralistas. We talked about the things we had to do, the kind of energy that had to be dealt with. We knew that we had to deal with a work load that was going to be tremendous, and that there would be the pressure of having no money. If people came to work with us because they thought they were going to get rich, they would have to forget about it! We had to think about the kinds of things we were contributing to the community. We didn't have a leader or director. We coordinated everything and worked as a cooperative group.

We talked about why we were painting murals and that in itself brought us together as a group, as a women's group. We wanted to be the ones to determine what was going to be on that wall. We wanted to have values as a group and to make our own statement rather than following the leader. Because we all knew each other and were friends, we understood our mutual feelings and needs.

The first mural we painted was the Model Cities Mural. It is 76 feet long and 24 feet wide and it is the largest mural that has been painted in the Mission community. *Pan America* is the theme for this mural, and at least four different countries or major areas in Latin America are represented in it. We found self-expression in a decorative design from these cultures. We did research in the maguey plant and on maize (corn), and learned the historical significance of these crops. We became knowledgeable about the colors and clothes that the figures in the mural are wearing. We collectivized our work, and within a month our design was complete.

Irene Pérez painted the magueys and the maize. Graciela Carillo painted Guatemala. Consuelo Mendez painted the center of the mural, which is the family unit, and Venezuela. I painted Bolivia and Peru. If you see the mural you'll notice all of the symbolism.

Q. What is the importance of the Mujeres Muralistas in the Chicana art movement?

A. I think Mujeres Muralistas is very important because we are a beginning of an art movement for women muralists. Ten years from now, if someone analyzes the significance of our work, they will see the step that we took forward as muralists. I think we are more Chicanas than women. The strength of our cultural heritage speaks more effectively for our womanhood. We have gone through a lot and have gained recognition, and this has proved our capabilities. Hopefully our murals speak for our people, and of the Chicano struggle. At this time in history our work is important because there are no other Chicana artists who have done such extensive work in the community on such a large scale and without pay. In the 1970s we have been able to express ourselves because there have been scholarships to assist Third World people. This has also been the time of recognition for us; the word "Chicano" has become powerful. Mexican-Americans of older generations have begun to accept our heritage, too.

Hopefully with the kind of work the Mujeres Muralistas have done, we can encourage more Chicana artists to take initiative as individuals to further their artwork. We have to be persistent because it is a struggle, especially with our economic background. Being a Chicana artist is definitely a struggle, and sacrifices must be made.

Currently I'm doing research on Chicana and Chicano artists, and I find very little listed. I'm sure there are many Chicana artists, but they haven't surfaced, and are not in the public view. As artists we should be able to show our work. We thrive off the public. The exposure of our work to the public can generate a sense of purpose for our self-expression.

Q. Do you think more Chicana artists will become involved in painting community murals and in other areas of art in the future?

A. I hope so. Right now there are very few. We should continue to struggle and persist, no matter what field of endeavor we are in. We should hang on because it's possible for us to achieve success. Maybe we won't become famous, and maybe we won't become rich, but we can let the world know that we are capable. ▪

An Interview with Wifredo Lam (1982)

In this excerpted interview from 1982, shortly before his death, Cuban artist Wifredo Lam talks about his identity as an Afro-Cuban painter. Lam discusses some of the symbolism in his painting La jungle (The Jungle)*, and the clearly anticolonial sentiment expressed in the artwork. The painter also references his relationship with Picasso and the influence of European avant-garde styles in his work.*

Source: "Genesis of *La jungla*: An Interview with Wifredo Lam," in *Manifestos and Polemics in Latin American Modern Art*, ed. and trans. Patrick Frank (Albuquerque: University of New Mexico Press, 2017), 84–86. Copyright © 2017 University of New Mexico Press.

They used to call me, in discriminatory terms, a black painter. In this, they showed their inability to obstruct the path that I had taken. The well-off are too weak in spirit to appreciate true art. I could say, along with [Francis] Picabia: "I will die content because my works have not pleased those whom I detest." From my Paris days, I had an idea: to take African art and put it to work in its own environment, in Cuba. I wanted to express in a work the resistance and combative energy of my ancestors.

La jungla gives form to the revenge of a small Caribbean country, Cuba, against the colonizers. I placed the shears [in the upper right] as the symbol of the cutting necessary to resist all foreign impositions on Cuba, against all colonization. We are already big enough to march ahead without assistance: Here are the shears.

In *La jungla* the African myths function within the Cuban landscape of the cane field. Cuba's entire destiny down to the present has revolved around the cultivation of sugar cane and its economic ramifications. My conversations with Picasso showed me that it is necessary to use all intellectual manifestations to forward a truth. . . . I have been considered a painter of the School of Paris, and a surrealist painter, and I don't know what other tendency, but never as a representative of the painting that I actually do and that which I believe I reflect in great measure: the poetry of the Africans who arrived in Cuba, and who still show so much pain in their songs and tales. I have put my feelings into forms, always following a poetic urgency. . . .

To paint *La jungla* I made maximum use of what I learned from studying the classics. And if that work is now widely renowned, it's because I did not paint it just casually, but rather seriously, with all my effort. I worked as if in a ritual, supported by my experiences in Spain and France. Into that work I put all my analytical abilities, which were never in conflict with my feelings. My interest in African and Polynesian art inspired me, and led me to unfold a series of subconscious motivations and observations; these did not follow sentimental pathways. I wanted to follow the insightful path opened by those primordial art forms, although without forgetting the compositional rigor that I had observed in Poussin and Cézanne.

An Interview with Oswaldo Guayasamín (1992)

Oswaldo Guayasamín (1919–99) was a master painter and sculptor from Ecuador, a country with large mestizo and Indigenous populations. Guayasamín is one of the few artists of Indigenous heritage in the Prado competition, and his work represents an important voice in the debates about how to define Latin American art. Guayasamín's paintings, which have been categorized as part of the Andean Indigenist movement, capture the political oppression, racism, poverty, and class division found throughout much of Latin America. This interview focuses on the Quincentenary activities that took place in Spain in 1992 to document and celebrate the 500 years since Columbus's arrival in America. Here the artist clearly expresses his disapproval toward the celebratory nature of the events in Spain and outlines a more critical perspective of the so-called discovery of a land that had been home to millions of Indigenous people long before the arrival of European explorers and colonizers. Guayasamín also develops his understanding of what it means to be "Latin American" and the role of art in this identity.

Source: Oswaldo Guayasamín, "Latin America Faces the Quincentenary: An Interview with Oswaldo Guayasamín," trans. Fred Murphy, *Latin American Perspectives* 9, no. 13 (Summer 1992): 101–3. Reproduced with permission of Sage Publications Inc. Journals through Copyright Clearance Center, Inc.

Interviewer (I): What position should Latin American intellectuals take toward the Quincentenary *[500th anniversary of Columbus landing in America]*?

Oswaldo Guayasamín (OG): I think any talk of celebration is really mistaken. How can we celebrate an event that was, at its own historic moment, so terrible and damaging for all our great pre-Columbian cultures? The humiliation, the slaughter of millions of Indians who were the owners of this continent makes this clear.

I: Some people are talking about the "encounter of two worlds" . . .

OG: Yes, but that's all just phraseology to justify the disastrous events for the continent.

I: What would be the proper term for it?

OG: I haven't thought about that, but the point is that America is fortunately now reacting in a powerful fashion. I have news from Mexico, Central America, Argentina, Bolivia, and Peru about persons who are working intensely to see that this event is not celebrated.

I: Isn't such a critical, emancipatory position going to cause problems for the official celebrations headed by Spain?

OG: It could cause difficulties. Here in Ecuador, for example—several years ago I made an immense statue of Rumiñahui, a hand-embossed bronze sculpture 8 meters high. We're now making the columns that will be placed behind this figure, columns nearly 20 meters high and covered with bronze, and a moveable sun. Rumiñahui is one of the greatest heroes of the pre-Columbian epoch; he defended the land, America's land, and carried on a fierce resistance from Cajamarca to Quito. For Latin America, Rumiñahui is one of the most important figures, and we're trying to inaugurate this monument in 1992. The idea of the Ministry of Education and Culture is to invite groups from all over the continent, from each country—dance troupes, music groups—not to celebrate but to protest, to integrate America, to realize once more the memory of what America was before the Spanish arrived.

I: In your paintings, you nearly always present a certain tragic, sad vision of Latin America. Is that the face of our identity?

OG: What I paint is not just linked to Latin America. The Age of Anger, [a series of works] which includes some 250 paintings, expresses all the tragedies of this century—the concentration camps, World War II, the Spanish Civil War, the atomic bombs—but it also includes events in Latin America—the dictatorships of the Southern Cone, of Argentina, the one in Chile, the one in Uruguay. I am of course very much concerned with expressing these things as a rejection of all the violence that the incalculable forces of money have created in this world.

I: If you were to try to define Latin American identity, how would you do it?

OG: The basic idea for me is to begin slowly doing away with borders. I know that's quite a difficult thing, but at least reducing their importance ought to be the first step we take toward the integration of Latin America. We all know about the partition that occurred in America at Independence: this continent was cut into pieces, as if they were the private property of the independence figures of the time. Ecuador's border with Peru, with Colombia; Bolivia's border with Colombia—this is all badly done. We have the same cultural identity, but we are cut up. We followed the example of Europe, where borders were truly necessary—say, between Spain and France, between France and Germany, entire peoples with different languages, different conceptions of the world. Nonetheless, there they have practically done away with their borders. We, who have a cultural unity for 8,000 years from the Rio Bravo to Patagonia, remain divided. We speak the same language, we have the same religion from top to bottom, our aspirations as a continent, our poverty—that whole identity is cut in pieces. For me, the first step is to try to reduce the importance of borders and hope that someday they may disappear.

I: Do you think that brotherhood really exists among the Latin American peoples?

OG: With the borders in place, they teach us from childhood on to hate those on the other side, but that is a new and superficial lesson compared with teaching us to love our neighbors. It's virtually the same throughout the continent—Colombians and Venezuelans, Ecuadorians and Peruvians, Peruvians and Chileans—in the end, everyone has some artificially provoked grievance, and the armies of Latin America bear much of the blame for this disunity.

I: What is the role of art in the creation of, or the search for, Latin American identity?

OG: Being concerned with our own problems dates back to the early days of this century, with the advent of the great Mexican painters—Orozco, Rivera, Siqueiros—who were the first to concern themselves with Latin American realities. I think that while their styles were quite basic in plastic terms, there is now a continental movement with different expressions appropriate to our continent, there are numerous creators of art not only in painting but also in music: Villa-Lobos in Brazil, for example—all his great compositions are deeply linked to his people. The same can be said of Ginastera in Argentina and of the Mexicans who are involved in music, literature, and architecture. The great literary figures of our continent are being read and translated into nearly all the languages of the globe. ▪

An Interview with Vik Muniz (1998)

This interview with Vik Muniz provides a firsthand look at the concepts of artistic inspiration, influence, and art theory through the eyes of a contemporary Latin American artist. Born and raised in Brazil, but currently based in New York, Vik Muniz embodies the profile of a global contemporary artist and calls into question the notion of a singular label to classify art or artists.

Source: "Vik Muniz and Charles Ashley Stainback: A Dialogue," in *Seeing Is Believing* (Verona: Arena Editions, 1998), http://vikmuniz.net/library/vik-muniz-and-charles-ashley-stainback-a-dialogue. Vik Muniz text © 2023 Vik Muniz / Licensed by VAGA at Artists Rights Society (ARS), NY.

Charles A. Stainback (CS): For some individuals working with photographic imagery, the label "photographer" is less than desirable. They almost always prefer the label "artist." You, however, embrace the title of photographer and the photographic medium itself with great fervor, yet the work appears on first glance more closely aligned to our traditional notion of fine art. Do you see yourself as a photographic heretic or a shaman with a camera?

Vik Muniz (VM): I attended art school in São Paulo for a few years. None of the instructors there knew the work of Joseph Beuys or Bruce Nauman. We would sit for three hours at a time drawing and modeling geometric solids and nudes, and occasionally chat about Bernini or Tiepolo. The seeming mindlessness of those exercises taught me almost everything about artmaking that I use today. It taught me how to organize visual information in a hierarchical way, giving me a more detailed understanding of the mechanisms of representation. It also inspired in me a respect for craft and technique that I have many times tried to rid myself of, but obviously have failed. One can learn how to be a draftsman, a photographer, or a sculptor in school, but there is no way to teach someone how to become an artist. It would be like teaching someone to be sick or happy, or to be a good dice player. I am a photographer when I photograph, and a draftsman when I draw, but an artist is what I am always becoming.

CS: How much exposure to contemporary art did you have prior to coming to the United States in 1983? Did any particular artists/artworks stand out?

VM: In the 1970s, because of the military government in Brazil, intellectuals lived in constant fear of being persecuted. Most of the music and art of that time is either camouflaged activism or corrupted by patriotism. There was always this lingering climate of a semiotic black market where hidden messages seemed encoded in every phrase: everything meant something else. People who carried books in their bags were considered a different kind of criminal by the semiliterate authoritarian police state, so reading books and hanging out with intellectuals was a way of being rebellious. That atmosphere gave me a chronic allergy to slogans and a clear vision of how information can be manipulated to serve certain ends. For obvious reasons, in those days I thought political art to be a government thing and abstract art to be for people who never walked the streets. I liked drawing the old paintings at the museum and didn't give much thought to contemporary art. The first contemporary artist I met was [José] Leonilson. In 1979 we were both helping the experimental theater group Asdrubal Trouxe o Trombone during their stint in São Paulo. I worked with him designing a poster and I told him that the boat he drew was crooked. He told me that the boat was crooked because that boat was his own. Leonilson made things that were infused with fragility and ambiguity, one of the very first Brazilian artists to show that side of an art object. He was an extraordinary artist and a great person. I miss him a lot.

CS: You seem to draw many of your ideas, or at least your inspiration, from art history, in particular those artists and works that have seemingly been of little significance, or at least overlooked by much of the contemporary art world. Where would you place your work in today's art world, an arena that puts such a huge premium on theoretical discourse?

VM: I'd rather say that I sometimes make work based on "old pictures" than on art history, which in general implies that there are some things to be considered before a certain work is perceived by the eye. I am more inclined to work with anonymous pieces because they are less polluted by historical information than masterworks. I've never taken a class in art history and sometimes think I'm very fortunate to have learned art by responding to pictures at a very personal level. The work of art that changed my life and prompted me to become an artist was a painting of a slightly cross-eyed girl whose facial asymmetry made the painting look alive. Her name was Clara Serena and it was just a coincidence that her father, the painter who executed the portrait, was Peter Paul Rubens.

I tend to like works from periods when new media emerge, forcing the existing ones to change. Early nineteenth-century painting, sculpture, and photography; impressionism; photography and painting between the wars—these are works that I am always scrutinizing. One day I was looking at a book by Sister Wendy and saw this very sweet portrait of Saint John the Baptist and a lamb done by Murillo. I have no idea why, but the silly little picture brought tears to my eyes. If I had studied art history and learned how corny Murillo was, I would have been deprived of that poignant experience. I have done some pictures after better-known works, but tried to play down their iconographic value by emphasizing their perceptual output. I did Leonardo's *Last Supper*, for example, but I wasn't thinking of Leonardo. I was thinking of perspective and the idea of the Eucharist as an early form of broadcasting. As for theory, I think that the only bad thing about art criticism is that it makes possible art about criticism. I like reading philosophy and history books. I even have an interest in neurology, psychology, and physics. But when I want to read something that will ultimately influence my work, I pick up a novel or book of poetry.

CS: Besides cleaning up all the messes you make, you also teach. Photography? Drawing and painting? It must be a great class and I would love to see the supply list you pass out at the beginning of the year.

VM: One of my greatest heroes is John Dewey, who always spoke of the individual's responsibility to pass on one's experience in the form of education. I teach photography, and drawing for photographers. (I do that more often than I clean up after myself.) Teaching, like writing and editing, is another way to pass on to others things that I consider important for everybody. I am always thinking of the responsibility—which we all have—to leave something for others. Recently, I began some research in the field of education concerning the development of programs for teaching visual literacy to children. There is very little being done in that area. It is important to teach kids the visual grammar behind the images they so readily consume. As images become increasingly more eloquent than the text that accompanies them, visual literacy becomes as important as reading itself. My classes have nothing to do with what I make.

I don't tell them to bring mustard, gunpowder, and maple syrup to class (although they do anyway). The school is where I vent those formless ideas and go wild about the immateriality of things. It saves me the trouble of having to cover that in my work. It also keeps me from making art that is didactic. I want these things to be beautiful, and I want this beauty to conceal the rhetoric behind them. ▪

An Interview with Fernando Botero (ca. 2000)

In this wide-ranging interview with Cristina Carrillo, the Colombian artist Fernando Botero talks about his personal aesthetic, his love of collecting art, and the future of painting. Published as part of a museum exhibition catalog, the interview marks the occasion of Botero's large donation of his privately owned paintings, collected throughout the years, to his home country. Botero's answers reveal his confident personality and his personal aesthetic preferences. Notice Botero's references to his private pre-Columbian art collection. What does this show about his understanding and appreciation of Indigenous culture in Latin America? What do Botero's answers reveal about the artist's opinions about private versus public art?

Source: "Entrevista con Fernando Botero," interview by Cristina Carrillo de Albornoz, in *Donación Botero: Colección Banco de la República* (Santafe de Bogotá, Colombia, 2000), 27–30. Translated by Bridget V. Franco.

Cristina Carrillo (CC): Could you tell us how you define your particular aesthetic?

Fernando Botero (FB): My collection, like all collectors, begins with having a work of art that I like on the main wall of my house. In my case, as an artist, I favor figurative painting, which should have a balance between the decorative and expressive elements, because when I look at a painting by Piero della Francesca, for example, I am struck by the beauty of the colors, the perfect equilibrium of the composition, the unexpected distribution of elements and the harmony of color, but at the same time the work says something to me beyond the formal aspects of the painting. It conveys something poetic, about human grandeur, with its gestures and solemnity. For these reasons, I was never a fervent supporter of abstraction, which, despite being very decorative, doesn't go beyond the formal.

CC: How would you describe yourself as a collector? How does being a painter influence you too?

FB: I am a painter who without realizing it became a collector too. Being an artist-collector, perhaps not as common nowadays, is an advantage because my profession has "trained my eye" to distinguish between a good piece of art and a mediocre one. But when collecting art, there are two factors that determine a collection: the availability of the artworks and the price. A collector buys what is available in the market and what he can afford. His selections do not necessarily demonstrate his favorite piece of art or artist, but rather they demonstrate that he was interested in a particular painting given the limitations of what was available and what he could afford.

CC: You have been collecting art for twenty-five years. How exactly did you begin? How did the idea of creating a collection come about? What was the first piece of art that you acquired?

FB: Actually I began collecting more than twenty-five years ago. During the 1960s, through my friend and fellow collector Checa Solaris, I acquired a series of paintings by Colombian and Peruvian artists from Latin America's colonial period. Later I lost interest in these pieces and I gave many of them away as gifts. During this same time, I began to collect pre-Columbian art. Thanks to a great art dealer who has passed away . . . , I was able to create a beautiful collection of these pieces that I still maintain, housed almost in its entirety in several of my residences. Afterwards I became interested in twentieth-century drawings, exchanging my own work for them on many occasions, or buying them in galleries or auctions. And I have tried to improve my collection through other changes. Sometimes you tire of a particular work and you trade it as part of the payment for a better piece by the same artist or a different one. This is one of the fun aspects of collecting. The oil paintings came later, starting with the artists whom I have always admired, in order to fill up the empty space on the walls. But I believe that true collectors buy art for the simple fact of possessing it, even when they run out of places to hang the works. It becomes an uncontrollable vice. . . .

CC: The world of art collecting is a unique universe, almost a secret one; do you view it this way?

FB: Yes, in some ways it is a secret world, given that you only show the artwork that you have hanging on the walls of your house, and the rest is a private universe, housed in warehouses that specialize in art conservation, where only the collector has access.

CC: Your collection begins with the impressionists. How are they represented in the collection and what fascinates you about that particular moment in art history?

FB: Many of them, the great majority, are represented in the collection. Impressionist painting is tremendously plastic, juicy, with very attractive daytime color and, perhaps, it is the direct way in which the artists have made their paintings that has seduced the entire world. The impressionists created a very clear language that clashed with the way things were painted previously, in other words, [French Academy] Salon painting. The impressionists have captivated the world, perhaps for their themes which are inspired in real life but treated poetically, or perhaps for their form which is so sensual and fresh. I think that the power of seduction comes from the unfinished sensation they transmit. In all of the impressionists' work there is a game of seduction with the public, a sense of wanting to be there.

CC: The rest of your collection is a journey through art of the twentieth century. In this new millennium do you have the sense that everything that could have been expressed has already been said? In your opinion, what is the most important revolution of the twentieth century?

FB: Human capacity for expression is infinite and twentieth-century art has expressed so much; there have been all kinds of schools, from the most realist to the most abstract. The biggest revolutions or influences were those of Cézanne in his last paintings, which already suggest abstract art and cubism, as well as Monet and his water lilies which created a new concept of space; because in these paintings the theme and the background don't exist but rather the whole canvas is an unlimited space, a general vibration. Black art, of course, through Picasso and his great freedom for the expression of nature, also marked this past century.

CC: What aspects of art from this century interest you the most and which ones have been the least fortunate?

FB: I have been most interested in figurative painters who create nature using a personal language because for me that is what art is: saying the same thing in a different way. It will always be the same tree, the same man, the same horse, the same mountain . . . seen in a different way through the artist's personality. Current artistic production is less intriguing to me because it tries to run away from the essence of painting itself: sculptural expression on a flat surface. Video, installations, are of course forms of artistic expression, like cinema and photography, but they are closer to the realm of theater and I don't think they can replace painting.

CC: Where is art headed? What is the future?

FB: Art will be more and more the result of individual personalities, personal expression. It is not possible to find new schools of art that are radically different because the most extreme realism or hyperrealism and the most abstract styles already exist. The future will oscillate between those two poles and then painters with personality who express reality in unique ways will return. At the end of the day, personal visions of the world are what the history of painting has traced—painters who have said the same thing but expressed it in diverse ways. The future will return to what art has always been, an expression of personalities. ▪

POEMS AND MISCELLANEOUS

Oswald Andrade, "Atelier [Art Studio]" (1925)

Brazilian writer Oswald Andrade penned this tribute to his wife and muse Tarsila do Amaral in the early 1920s. The poem takes its title from the French word for art studio, "atelier," and signals the various tensions that characterized the modernist debate in Latin America: rural versus urban, local versus cosmopolitan, Brazilian versus European, the slow pace of country life versus rapid industrialization. The poem celebrates the Brazilian artist (referred to here as a caipirinha, or country girl) in her duality as a local country girl who is dressed in an expensive gown by Parisian designer Paul Poiret.

Source: Oswald Andrade, "Atelier" (1925), trans. Graham Howells, in *Tarsila do Amaral* (Madrid: Fundación Juan March, 2009), 96.

ART STUDIO

Caipirinha dressed by Poiret
São Paulo laziness lives in your eyes
That have never seen Paris nor Piccadilly
Nor the compliments of men
In Seville
As you passed between earrings

National trains and creatures
Geometrize the clear atmosphere
Congonhas pales under the pall
Of processions in Minas
The greenness in the klaxon blue
Cut
On the red dust

Skyscrapers
Fords
Viaducts
A smell of coffee
In the framed silence ▪

Xul Solar, "Neocriollo Glossary" (1931)

Xul Solar was fluent in at least ten languages, and his vision of a utopia focused on the creation of a universal language. Believing Spanish to be several centuries out of date, marred by words that were too long and too cacophonous, he invented neocriollo *(neocreole) in 1920. It was derived from Spanish and Portuguese, with bits of French, English, and Guaraní, and meant to be a universal language for the entire South American continent. The following condensed glossary contains some useful* neocriollo *words that you may want to learn so that you can communicate with Sr. Solanas, the art dealer for Xul Solar's painting.*

In Xul Solar's Spanish translations, note that he consistently omits the vowel u *after* q, *a reflection of his tendency to reduce words to their basic elements.*

Source: *"Apuntes de Neocriollo,"* Azul: Revista de Ciencias y Letras *2, no. 11 (August 1931): 201–5. Translated by Bridget V. Franco.*

Esto está en criol, o neocriollo, futur lenguo del Contenente. *[This is in Creolo, or Neo-Creole, the future language of the Continent.]* ▪

Neocriollo	Spanish	English translation
xu	su; dellos	theirs
sür	sobre, super	over
g'ral	en general	generally speaking
man	humano	human
chi	chico	boy; small
bau	edificio, constru'	building, construction
plur	plural, múltiple	plural, multiple
pli	complíqido, complejo	complicated
dootri	en otra parte	somewhere else
Bria	mundo almi	world of souls
per	qe dura, continuo	that which lasts; continual
fon	fónico, qe suena	related to sound; that which makes sounds
kin	kinético, qe se mueva	kinetic, that which moves
pir	de fuego, de ardor	fire
c'len	caliente, de calor	warm
sui	especial, a su modo	special, in his/her own way
tro	trop, demasiado	too much
epi, 'pi	encima	on top of
tun	temporario, provisiorio	temporary, provisional

Frida Kahlo, Diary Entry (ca. 1944)

This entry from Frida Kahlo's personal diary reveals the artist's strong emotions toward and complex relationship with her husband, fellow Mexican artist Diego Rivera, whom Kahlo married in 1929 at the young age of twenty-two, divorced ten years later, and then remarried in 1940. Kahlo and Rivera's relationship was tumultuous, marked by infidelity, jealousy, passionate political debates, and serious illness. The handwritten diary entries, accompanied many times by colorful drawings and sketches that reveal Kahlo's inner world, were written over the period of a decade, from approximately 1944 until her untimely death in 1954. One of the noteworthy concepts that Kahlo expresses in her diary entries is the idea that Rivera is the auxócromo *(the one who captures or sees color), and she is the* cromóforo *(the one who brings or gives color)—together they form a symbiotic relationship that informs their artistic, psychic, and physical worlds. In this poetic example, Kahlo lists the many different identities and roles that Rivera fulfills, before ultimately concluding that any attempt to define or possess the object of her love is useless, as he belongs to himself, not to her.*

Source: Frida Kahlo, *El diario de Frida Kahlo: Un íntimo autorretrato* (Ciudad de México: La Vaca Independiente, 2019), 235 [lámina 60]. Translated by Bridget V. Franco.

Diego principio	Diego beginning
Diego constructor	Diego builder
Diego mi niño	Diego my boy
Diego mi novio	Diego my boyfriend
Diego pintor	Diego painter
Diego mi amante	Diego my lover
Diego "mi esposo"	Diego "my husband"
Diego mi amigo	Diego my friend
Diego mi madre	Diego my mother
Diego mi padre	Diego my father
Diego mi hijo	Diego my son
Diego = Yo =	Diego = Me =
Diego Universo	Diego Universe
Diversidad en la unidad	Diversity in unity

Por qué le llamo *mi* Diego?	Why do I call him *my* Diego?
Nunca fue ni será mío.	He never was nor ever will be mine.
Es de él mismo.	He belongs to himself.

David A. Siqueiros, *How to Paint a Mural* (1951)

This heavily excerpted text from several chapters of Mexican muralist David A. Siqueiros's How to Paint a Mural *(1951) outlines the parameters for a successful mural project. Siqueiros grounds the instructions in his 1949 experience in San Miguel de Allende, Mexico, where he and his team set out to create a mural dedicated to the life of General Ignacio Allende, a historical figure in Mexico's struggle for independence, on the walls of the eighteenth-century ex-convent of Santa Rosa. Siqueiros painstakingly documents eighteen steps, each with its own chapter, to create a large-scale mural painting on an existing building. The book touches on the history of Italian fresco painting, linking the Renaissance tradition to the Mexican muralist movement that emerged in the 1920s. Many of the chapters read like a textbook or manual, covering technical topics like spatial geometry, how to mix materials for paint, and the challenges of painting on polyangular surfaces. Unfortunately, despite his own expert advice on how to paint a mural, Siqueiros's work on the project, titled* Monumento al capitán General Ignacio Allende, *was interrupted, and the mural remains unfinished to this day.*

Source: David A. Siqueiros, *How to Paint a Mural* (*Cómo se pinta un mural*) (1951), in *Art and Revolution*, trans. Sylvia Calles (London: Lawrence and Wishart, 1975), 102–37. Reproduced with permission of Lawrence and Wishart Limited through PLSclear.

The Importance of Team Work

It is obvious that a mural painting, because of its size cannot be carried out by one man alone; you cannot be an individual work of art. Easel painting is, by its very nature, individual.

It is therefore quite difficult for painters whose mental structure has been formed by easel painting to understand what we might call the collective painter.

. . . my later experiences in painting murals, in Los Angeles, California, gave me some practical experience which on the one hand dispelled my mystical ideas about directorless team work, and on the other hand inspired me to work in the team. This is the only type of work which can teach the art of mural painting. I allowed my collaborators, both teachers and pupils, to learn for themselves. Since we all knew beforehand of the subject of the mural, I allowed them to start tracing directly on the wall.

What was the result? In the first place, we found we needed a director, in the same way as an orchestra needs a conductor. In the second place, we noticed that each one tended to apply his own style. And in the third place, we discovered that no matter how good the drawing might be, it was no good for mural painting unless it conformed strictly to the mural method of polyangular drawing.

In painting a mural, all the painters form a team and that team must only have one director. The director, who should be the most experienced painter, should, when the fundamental bases of the work are decided, encourage and coordinate the creative contribution of all the others.

Understanding the Geometric Structure of the Architect

. . . the architect's geometric structure must be thoroughly understood . . . we should closely observe the room while walking both fast and slowly, and this is of vital importance. By studying the height of the walls, the relationship between the walls and the vaulted ceiling, the inter-spatial relationship between the arches, vaults, walls and floor, we came to understand the marvelous play of space in the room where we were to paint our mural.

Function and Subject Should Be Decided by the Team

By choosing a historical subject in a place which was so important in the fight for Mexico's independence did we help our art in any way? Was it an arbitrary act to get a group of young artists, most of them foreign, to spend time on this study? Would it perhaps have been better to take as a subject for our mural something which was not related to history and had no ideological content? The decision to give our mural a political function . . . was unanimous. We resolved to link the plastic beauty, rhythm, geometrical movement, colour relationships, and the play of textures, expressions and pictorial psychology to a utilitarian purpose. Had we not done so we would have been guilty of ridiculous escapism.

We would decide our style during the course of the work; we would trust to our own perception and rational consideration of the problem, based on the reactions of the public. Art, we said, is produced both by the artist and his audience simultaneously, and we added: art must be suited to the audience. This is why art was great when it had a great audience, and was poor when its audience was socially restricted.

The Fundamental Tracing: Composition

We have already decided on the function of the room we are to decorate, we have decided on the subject, and made a historical study of it, we have collected graphic material to illustrate our historical study, we have produced sketches and photographs. Now we must proceed to make a photographic analysis of the polyangular distortions of each area. When this has been done, we must start tracing on the walls. In mural painting, more than in any other kind of painting, we must go from the general to the particular. In mural painting, the main emphasis should be placed on the primary volumes as a structural base for subsequent details. The distance from which our mural is to be viewed requires that superfluous elements should be eliminated.

From Tracing to Colour

My practice has led me to the conclusion that the preparatory organization of space should not be limited to the lineal tracing, but that immediately afterwards masses or flat areas of colour must be applied because (and this is one of the things which have been rediscovered by the abstractionists of the cosmopolitan School of Paris) colour has a spatial value, since it gives different depths.

As we began to apply the colour I called the students' attention to an interesting phenomenon: the luminous colours (for example the golden ochres) seemed further from our eyes than the browns and siennas. Quite often the warm colours, those in which red predominates (the cold colours are those in which blue predominates), appeared further away than the others, which according to our traditional ideas are supposedly atmospheric.

What could this be due to? When will the *experts* help us to understand this scientifically? I think I can put forward the following theory: *colours have no autonomous value nor belligerency of their own; they only live through chromatic relationships with the colours around them.*

It is perfectly obvious that when blue is surrounded by reds it is not the same as a blue surrounded by greens and yellows, even though it is physically the same colour. I cannot say any more about the use of colour, because colour is an intensely personal thing and you can no more theorise about colour than you can tell a person how to draw.

Supervising the Photogenic Quality of the Work

On the principle that our work is a public form of art, we must see that it reaches as many people as possible. We can therefore say (begging the pardon of those who believe in the mystique of aesthetics) that, in the last report, mural painting must be photogenic, i.e. easily photographed in black and white, so that it is not limited to the physical place where it is painted and can be circulated to a wider audience. And only in this way will it be really public.

In the future, cinematography will be of the utmost importance in photographing murals. The cine camera can reproduce *visual truth*, and that is the *pictorial truth* of mural painting; because of its power to move, it can reconstruct in a given architectonic photograph the normal active process of the spectator, which was the basis of the painting's composition. If the film is made in colour (and there is no doubt that black and white will disappear just as the silent cinema has done) then the mural will have been totally reproduced for circulation to the people. ▪

Street Art Group, "Methodologies" (2009)

"Methodologies" outlines some of the characteristics and concepts that define and drive the artistic and political work of the Street Art Group (Grupo de Arte Callejero, GAC). This excerpt describes the group's working dynamics, which prioritize collectivity and playfulness, and criticizes the Western idea of primary, individual authorship in the production of art.

Source: Grupo de Arte Callejero, "Metodologías," in *Pensamientos, prácticas y acciones del GAC* (Buenos Aires: Tinta Limón, 2009), 179–82. Translated by Bridget V. Franco.

What do we do? How do we do it? How do we think about what we do? For each of these questions, there could be a multitude of different answers because we do not have just one way of handling our artistic production in this group; we don't even have a unifying outlook about the "what" or the "how," and this is something that fluctuates with time anyway. No one moment of production is the same as another, and the things we construct as discourse do not mean the same thing in different moments and places.

So, the questions should be: What common characteristics can we detect in the diversity of our work?

Work within the Group

- Working dynamics: meetings, round table discussions, confrontation, consensus as the result of tensions between individualities
- How are power relationships articulated and taken apart from within
- Affective

Formats

Visual interventions and, within these, the presence of graphic imagery. / Performative actions, "whole body." / Playfulness as a work incentive and as a mechanism for engaging with others. / Direct action vs. long-term projects, which demonstrate the process of creation itself.

DRAMATIC VS. DISCREET

- The impact of size, quantity and proliferation of the object-image, as well as the high or low visibility of the body that intervenes in the space.
- The masses, holidays, protests, marches. Being inside, being outside. The minimal, the face to face.
- Visibility limits, where does the intervention begin and where does it end; the spectator's gaze that indicates what s/he sees, like a new text generated within the same context

EFFECTIVENESS VS. EFFICIENCY

- How do we think about these concepts from a communicative point of view?
- How do we imagine from the point of view of social transformation, or "changing minds"?
- What is our priority: quantity or quality? The massiveness of a discourse is not necessarily equal to its effectiveness.
- Depending on the particular instance, how can we measure this effectiveness, what are the signs? The importance of feedback.
- For whom are we talking, how do we think about "spectators"? Imagine them as active recipients, as co-participants in the construction of discourse. Or, imagine them as subjects of confrontation.

- Effectiveness measured within: in what sense does our work transform us.
- The urgency of speaking, when is it more important to "answer" quickly rather than go through a process of prior reflection, when does the reflection come after the action.

The Question of the Author

- The idea of intellectual property vs. collective creation and shared knowledge
- Anonymous character of certain productions
- The authorship of a particular action-intervention or image is reconfigured according to the context and the agents who were involved in its construction. There is no one author, only multiple, speaking identities, depending on each case
- The lack of signatures as a stimulus for re-appropriation
- When certain circuits require a signature: gallery exhibitions or lectures in institutional spaces
- Call into question the idea of originality, of "who thought of it first"
- Disagreement with the idea of the author as an intensification of the role of artist: the artist as an illuminating producer of symbols, as the one who possesses knowledge which s/he disseminates

Here we pause to clarify our position, because it is very common within the art world . . . to claim authorship of certain modes of creation. We believe that it is more productive to study the circumstantial characteristics that gave rise to similar productions in different periods, rather than simply place names on a time line. Furthermore, the prioritization of authorship as a mechanism of validation does not contribute to the reflection about what has been done in the work, on the contrary: it makes the marginalized of history permanently invisible. This attitude is influenced by the prevalence of the concept of "aura" and by the concept of "work of art," both of which nullify the interactions between artistic and political practices. ▪

Acknowledgments

RTTP games are never created in isolation or developed in a vacuum. Many people have provided me with support, guidance, and motivation along the way, and I would like to give a special thanks to the following individuals:

Megan Sawicki, research assistant, for her in-depth research, acute problem-solving skills, and critical eye as we expanded and improved the game book and instructor's manual during the summer of 2017.

Lisa Crossman, PhD, curator of American art and arts of the Americas at the Mead Art Museum (Amherst College), for her feedback and enthusiastic support during the game development process.

Gretchen K. McKay and Nicolas W. Proctor, co-authors of the *Modernism vs. Traditionalism: Art in Paris, 1888–89*, game for their suggestions, support, and permission to include their primer on the formal elements of art in this book.

All my *Prado* play-testers from the 2016 Game Development Conference at Central Michigan University, especially Jon Truitt, Nick Proctor, Mary Jane Treacy, Mary Beth Looney, Marie Gasper-Hulvat, Jeffrey Hyson, and Stephany Slaughter.

Anne Caillaud, Janel Pettes-Guikema, and David Eick of Grand Valley State University for their helpful suggestions about integrating RTTP in the foreign-language curriculum. Terri Nelson of California State University, San Bernardino, for her detailed game review, enthusiastic support, and helpful suggestions.

All my students at the College of the Holy Cross who have play-tested the *Prado* game in-person and virtually, especially in my Montserrat seminars, and my colleagues in the Spanish Department who have "played" along and supported game-based learning pedagogy, especially Professors Helen Freear-Papio, Daniel Frost, Rodrigo Fuentes, and Cynthia Stone.

My deepest appreciation to the instructors at other institutions who have play-tested the *Prado* game in their classes, in English and Spanish, and shared their invaluable feedback for improving the game: Stephany Slaughter (Alma College), Zulema Moret, Médar Serrata, and Elizabeth Gansen (Grand Valley State University), Sandra Sousa (University of Central Florida), Rhonda L. Reymond (West Virginia University), Alice Bendinelli (Southwestern College, Kansas), and Terri Nelson (California State University, San Bernardino).

Thanks to Andrew Winters and Mary Carley Caviness at the University of North Carolina Press and copyeditor Christi Stanforth for their guidance and editorial support during the final stages of publication.

Finally, Samuel, Lucía, and Santiago—true gamers who, while they may never read a page of this book, embody the spirit of joyful and uninhibited play as they make their way through the world. Thank you for reminding me how powerful and beautiful your imagination can be.

The development of this game has been made possible by funding from:

Weiss Summer Research in the Humanities, Social Sciences and Arts Program and the George I. Alden Trust, College of the Holy Cross (Summer 2017).

Teaching Institutes and Conferences Travel Grant, Center for Teaching, College of the Holy Cross, to attend the RTTP Faculty Institute at Barnard College (2015, 2018) and the Game Development Conference at Central Michigan University (2016).

Summer Course Development Faculty Fellowship for Integration of RTTP in SPAN 301, Office for the Vice President for Academic Affairs, College of the Holy Cross (2016).

Faculty Publication Award, Committee on Faculty Scholarship, College of the Holy Cross (2023).

Appendix
Recursos en español (Spanish-Language Resources)

ELEMENTOS FORMALES

La línea es el primero y el más versátil de los elementos visuales del arte. El espectador puede tener una reacción psicológica a diferentes tipos de línea:

La línea curveada sugiere la comodidad y la facilidad.
La línea horizontal sugiere distancia y tranquilidad.
La línea vertical sugiere altura y fuerza.
La línea zigzag sugiere caos y ansiedad.

La forma puede ser normal o irregular, plano (dos dimensiones) o sólido (tres dimensiones), representativa o abstracta, geométrica u orgánica, transparente u opaca, decorativa o simbólica. Las siguientes formas geométricas pueden influir la reacción del espectador:

Los cuadros y rectángulos pueden representar fuerza y estabilidad.
Los círculos y óvalos pueden representar el movimiento continuo.
Los triángulos guían el ojo hacia arriba.
Los triángulos invertidos pueden crear una sensación de tensión y desbalance

El tono es la calidad clara u oscura de los colores. El tono se usa para crear:

un contraste de iluminación y oscuridad
un ambiente tranquilo o dramático
una sensación de profundidad y distancia

El color es el elemento visual que tiene el efecto más fuerte sobre nuestras emociones. Aquí hay algunos asociaciones y simbolismos cromáticos:

rojo: pasión, violencia, peligro, enojo, aventura; llama la atención
azul: color del mar y del cielo; frío y lento en contraste al rojo; el tono de azul determina su significado:
—azul oscuro: confianza, dignidad, inteligencia
—azul claro: eternidad, paz, serenidad, espiritualidad
amarillo: el color más luminoso del espectro cromático; alegría, calor, optimismo, creatividad; pero también puede simbolizar precaución, locura, enfermedad. En México el color amarillo brillante se asocia con la muerte.
anaranjado: vibrante, caliente, fuego. Simboliza energía, vitalidad, buena salud. Es un color que polariza al espectador.
verde: crecimiento, fertilidad, renacimiento; asociado con la naturaleza y con la ecología
morado, violeta, púrpura: no es un color natural común; la rareza del morado le ha dado un aura de lujo e importancia. Asociado con la nobleza, energía sobrenatural, luto

La textura es la calidad de la superficie de una composición artística—la característica áspera o suave, lisa del material usado para crear la imagen. Experimentamos textura ópticamente (crea la ilusión de textura con la vista) y físicamente, es decir, el material usado (la tela, la pintura, la madera, la brocha) crea una textura palpable.

Lines are the primary and most versatile visual elements of art. Different kinds of lines can produce emotional or psychological reactions in the viewer:

Curved lines suggest comfort and ease.
Horizontal lines suggest distance and tranquility.
Vertical lines suggest height and strength.
Zigzag lines suggest chaos and anxiety.

Forms can be regular or irregular, flat (two-dimensional), or solid (three-dimensional), representative or abstract, geometric or organic, transparent or opaque, decorative or symbolic. The following geometric forms can guide the viewer's reaction:

Squares and rectangles can represent strength and stability.
Circles and ovals can represent continual movement.
Triangles guide the viewer's eye upward.
Inverted triangles can create a sense of tension and imbalance.

Tone is the light and dark quality of colors. Tone is used to create:

contrast between light and darkness;
peaceful or dramatic atmosphere; and
sensations of profundity and distance

Color is the visual element that has the strongest effect on our emotions. Here are some chromatic associations and symbolism.

red: passion, violence, danger, anger, adventure, attention
blue: color of the sea and the sky; cold and slow compared to red; the tone of a blue can determine its meaning:
—dark blue: confidence, dignity, intelligence;
—light blue: eternity, peace, serenity, spirituality

yellow: the brightest color of the chromatic scale; connotes happiness, warmth, optimism, creativity; but yellow can also symbolize caution, madness, sickness. In Mexico, bright yellow is associated with death.
orange: vibrant, warm, fire. Orange symbolizes energy, vitality, good health. A color that polarizes or focuses the viewer.
green: growth, fertility, rebirth; associated with nature and the environment
purple, violet: not a common natural color; the rare quality of purple gives it an aura of luxury and importance. Associated with nobility, supernatural energy, mourning

Texture is the quality of the surface in an artistic composition—the softness, roughness, smoothness of the material used to create the image. We experience texture optically (creates the visual illusion of texture) and physically, in other words, the material (fabric, paint, wood, brush) creates a palpable texture on the canvas.

VOCABULARIO BÁSICO DE ARTE
Palabras básicas para transmitir los conceptos generales.

el/la autor/a: artista. Persona que se dedica a crear arte de manera profesional o como aficionado.
corriente: tendencia artística que siguen diferentes personas, siempre con rasgos comunes en su trabajo. También se puede llamar "movimiento."
cromático: relativo a los colores de un cuadro. Por ejemplo: *El valor cromático del cuadro es muy elevado.*
marchante: una persona que vende obras de arte; del francés *marchand*
obra: cada uno de los trabajos artísticos de una persona. Puede referirse a cualquier área (música, escultura, pintura, etc.).
técnica: conjunto de habilidades, utensilios y conocimientos aplicados a las obras. Por ejemplo, la acuarela es una técnica y el óleo es otra.

También puedes introducir en tus discursos estos verbos relacionados con el arte.

colorear: dar color a una obra, con el uso de pigmentos, tintes, ceras o cualquier material adecuado en cada caso

esbozar: dibujar contornos, hacer un bosquejo poco definido

dibujar: trazar formas y figuras sobre una superficie

delinear: trazar líneas para obtener una figura, generalmente en planos de dibujo técnico

pintar: representar algo en una superficie con líneas y colores

BASIC ART VOCABULARY (TRANSLATION)

author: artist, person who creates art professionally or as an amateur

trend: general style or tendency with common characteristics implemented by different people; can also be called "movement"

chromatic: relating to the colors in a painting. For example: *The chromatic value of the painting is intense.*

art dealer: a person who sells artwork; comes from the French *marchand [merchant]*

work, art work: each individual piece of art by an artist; can refer to any artistic area (music, sculpture, painting, etc.)

technique: combination of abilities, tools, and knowledge applied to artworks. For example, watercolor is one technique, and oil on canvas is another kind of technique.

You can also use these art-related verbs when talking about art.

to color: give color to an artwork, through the use of pigment, dye, waxes or other materials appropriate to each medium

to sketch: draw the contours of a shape, make an outline with few details or definition

to draw: create shapes and figures on a surface

to draft: draw lines to create a figure, generally as part of a technical drawing plan

to paint: depict something on a surface using lines and colors

EXPANDED ART VOCABULARY (BILINGUAL)

The following vocabulary in English and Spanish may be useful when describing a painting to others.

GENERAL VOCABULARY	VOCABULARIO GENERAL
the foreground	el primer plano
middle ground	el plano medio
background	el fondo
to be in the background	estar en el fondo
in the background	al fondo
the edge (top, bottom)	el borde (inferior, superior)
point of view	el punto de vista
brushstroke	la pincelada
uncomplete, unfinished	inacabado, incompleto
contrast with	contrastar con
bring out	resaltar, sacar a relucir, hacer notar
blur	desdibujar, hacer borroso
become blurred, get blurred	ponerse borroso
to fade away	desdibujarse, desvanecerse, difumarse
foreshorten	escorzar
depth	la profundidad
in the top left-hand corner	en el extremo superior izquierdo
in the bottom right-hand corner	en el extremo inferior derecho
at the center of the composition	en el centro de la composición
personify	personificar
stand for	representar
symbolize	simbolizar
portrait	el retrato
self-portrait	el autorretrato
everyday life scene	una escena de la vida cotidiana
still life	una naturaleza muerta, el bodegón
seascape	el paisaje marino
townscape, cityscape	el paisaje urbano
subject	el sujeto
theme	el tema
depict, show	mostrar
figure	la figura
standing	estar de pie
sitting	estar sentado/a
lying, reclined	estar recostado/a
kneeling	estar arrodillado/a
crouching	estar agachado/a

GENERAL VOCABULARY (*cont.*)	VOCABULARIO GENERAL (*cont.*)
leaning on	estar apoyado/a en
in profile	de perfil
line	la línea
form	la forma
tone	el tono
color	el color
texture	la textura
style	el estilo
space, volume	el espacio, el volumen
three-dimensional	tridimensional
two-dimensional	bidimensional
flat	plano/a
voluminous	voluminoso/a
perspective	la perspectiva
proportion	la proporción
curved line	línea curva
straight line	línea recta
wavy line	línea ondulada
rough	áspero/a, rugoso/a
smooth	suave, liso/a
even	balanceado/a, liso/a
uneven	desigual
sharp	afilado/a
blunt	desafilado/a
circle	círculo
circular	circular
cone	cono
cube	cubo
cubic	cúbico/a
cylinder	cilindro
cylindrical	cilíndrico/a
hexagon	hexágono
hexagonal	hexagonal
hollow	hueco/a
octagonal	octogonal
oval	óvalo, ovalado/a

COLORS	LOS COLORES
pink	rosa, rosado
green	verde
blue	azul
navy blue	azul marino
blue-green	azul verdoso
red	rojo
red-orange	rojo anaranjado
yellow	amarillo
yellow-orange	amarillo anaranjado
yellow-green	amarillo verdoso
orange	naranja
purple	púrpura, morado
violet	violeta
brown	marrón, café
chestnut	castaño
black	negro
white	blanco
golden	dorado
gray	gris
pale, light (for example, light green)	claro (por ejemplo, verde claro)
dark (for example, dark green)	oscuro (por ejemplo, verde oscuro)
warm colors	colores cálidos
cold colors	colores fríos
muted	apagado/a

TECHNIQUES AND MATERIALS	TÉCNICAS Y MATERIALES
brushstroke	la pincelada
canvas	el lienzo
engrave	grabar
paint	pintar
outline, draw	delinear
color	colorear
sketch	esbozar
carve, etch onto	grabar algo en
etching	el grabado
sculpture	la escultura
sculpt, carve	esculpir, entallar
skill	la habilidad, el talento, la destreza
treat	tratar
spray paint	pintar con aerógrafo
oil paint	pintura de óleo
oil on canvas	óleo sobre lienzo
acrylic paint	pintura acrílica
charcoal	el carboncillo
colored pencil	el lápiz de color
ink	la tinta
pastel	al pastel, tonos pastel
watercolor	la acuarela
drawing	el dibujo
painting	una pintura, un cuadro
sketch	el boceto, el bosquejo, el esbozo
mural	el mural
ceramics, pottery	la cerámica
architecture	la arquitectura
stained glass	el vitral
photography	la fotografía
performance	la representación, el espectáculo

ARTISTS	LOS ARTISTAS
studio	el taller, el estudio
throughout his/her career	a lo largo de su carrera
earlier work	una obra temprana
late work	una obra tardía
in the later part of his/her career	en la última fase de su carrera
masterpiece	una obra maestra
dedicate oneself to	dedicarse a
create	crear
complete, finish	completar, acabar, terminar
sculptor	el/la escultor/a
artist	el/la artista
painter	el/la pintor/a
achieve	lograr
achievement	el logro
his/her best achievement	su mayor logro, éxito
To treat	tratar
treatment, handling	el tratamiento
revolutionary, groundbreaking	revolucionario/a, innovador/a
experiment	un experimento
forerunner	el/la precursor/a
to foreshadow	presagiar
to found	fundar
the founder	el/la fundador/a
traditional	tradicional
conventional	convencional
mainstream	la corriente principal
rupture	una ruptura

THE MUSEUM	EL MUSEO
a visitor	un/a visitante
the catalog	el catálogo
catalog entry	una entrada del catálogo
entrance fee	la entrada
free admission	la entrada libre
a purchase	una adquisición, una compra
appraisal, valuation	la valuación, el avalúo
appraise, value, assess	tasar, valuar, avaluar
to commission a work	encargar una obra
a commission (from)	un encargo (de)
art critic	un/a crítico/a de arte
review of an exhibition	una reseña de una exhibición
curator	el/la curador/a
art dealer	el/la tratante de arte

Source: Created by and used with permission of Elizabeth Gansen, Grand Valley State University, Allendale, MI.

Bibliography

Agosin, Marjorie, ed. *A Woman's Gaze: Latin American Women Artists*. New York: White Pine, 1998.

Alejandro Xul Solar (1887–1963). New York: Rachel Adler Gallery, 1991.

Antliff, Mark, and Patricia D. Leighten. *Cubism and Culture*. London: Thames and Hudson, 2001.

Barnitz, Jacqueline, and Patrick Frank. *Twentieth-Century Art of Latin America*. Austin: University of Texas Press, 2015.

Botero, Fernando, and Werner Spies. *Fernando Botero: Paintings and Drawings*. Munich: Prestel, 1997.

Carter, Curtis L. *Wifredo Lam in North America*. Milwaukee: Patrick and Beatrice Haggerty Museum of Art, Marquette University, 2007.

Castedo, Leopoldo, and Phyllis Freeman. *A History of Latin American Art and Architecture: From Pre-Columbian Times to the Present*. New York: Praeger, 1969.

Colectivo Situaciones. *Genocide in the Neighborhood*. Translated by Brian Whitener, Daniel Borzutzky, and Fernando Fuentes. Oakland, CA: Chainlinks, 2009.

Congdon, Kristin G, and Kara K. Hallmark. *Artists from Latin American Cultures: A Biographical Dictionary*. Westport, CT: Greenwood, 2002.

Diego Rivera: A Retrospective, 1886–1957. New York: Detroit Institute of Arts, 1986. Exhibition catalog.

Feinstein, Hermine. "The Art Response Guide: How to Read Art for Meaning, a Primer for Art Criticism." *Art Education* 3 (1989): 43–53.

Frank, Patrick, ed. and trans. *Manifestos and Polemics in Latin American Modern Art*. Albuquerque: University of New Mexico Press, 2017.

———. *Readings in Latin American Modern Art*. New Haven, CT: Yale University Press, 2004.

Frida Kahlo, Diego Rivera, and Twentieth-Century Mexican Art: The Jacques and Natasha Gelman Collection. San Diego: Museum of Contemporary Art, 2000. Exhibition catalog.

Golding, John. *Cubism: A History and an Analysis, 1907–1914*. 3rd ed. Cambridge, MA: Harvard University Press, 1988.

Herbert, Robert L., ed. *Modern Artists on Art: Ten Unabridged Essays*. New York: Prentice Hall, 1986.

Jakovsky, Anatole. *Naive Painting*. Oxford: Phaidon, 1979.

Kahlo, Frida, and Erika Billeter. *The Blue House: The World of Frida Kahlo*. Frankfurt: Schirn Kunsthalle, 1993.

Kettenmann, Andrea. *Diego Rivera: A Revolutionary Spirit in Modern Art*. New York: Benedikt Taschen Verlag, 1997.

Kirstein, Lincoln. *The Latin-American Collection of the Museum of Modern Art*. New York: Museum of Modern Art, 1943.

Martinez, Soraida. *Soraida's Verdadism: The Intellectual Voice of a Puerto Rican Woman on Canvas. Unique, Controversial Images and Style*. Gibbsboro, NJ: Paint Works Corporate Center, 1999.

Mella, Joseph S., Carlos A. Jáuregui, and Edward F. Fischer, eds. *Of Rage and Redemption: The Art of Oswaldo Guayasamín*. Nashville: Center for Latin American and Iberian Studies at Vanderbilt University and the Vanderbilt University Fine Arts Gallery, 2008. Exhibition catalog.

Olea, Héctor, and Melina Kervandjian, eds. *Resisting Categories: Latin American and/or Latino?* Critical Documents of 20th-Century Latin American and Latino Art Series. Houston: Museum of Fine Arts, Houston, 2012.

Pérez, Sarduy P., and Jean Stubbs. *Afrocuba: An Anthology of Cuban Writing on Race, Politics and Culture*. Melbourne: Ocean Press, 1993.

Pinder, Kymberly N. *Race-ing Art History: Critical Readings in Race and Art History*. New York: Routledge, 2002.

Ramírez, Mari Carmen, and Héctor Olea. *Inverted Utopias: Avant-Garde Art in Latin America*. New Haven, CT: Yale University Press, 2004. Exhibition catalog.

Ramírez, Mari Carmen, and Marcelo Pacheco, eds. *Modern and Contemporary Masterworks from Malba—Museo de Arte Latinoamericano de Buenos Aires*. Houston: Museum of Fine Arts, Houston, 2012. Exhibition catalog.

Rasmussen, Waldo, Fatima Bercht, and Elizabeth Ferrer, eds. *Latin American Artists of the Twentieth Century*. New York: Museum of Modern Art, 1993. Exhibition catalog.

Schwartz, Jorge. *Las vanguardias latinoamericanas: Textos programáticos y críticos*. Madrid: Cátedra, 1991.

Stavans, Ilan, and Jorge J. E. Gracia. *Thirteen Ways of Looking at Latino Art*. Durham, NC: Duke University Press, 2014.

Sullivan, Edward J. *Latin American Art in the Twentieth Century*. London: Phaidon, 1996.

Unruh, Vicky. *Latin American Vanguards: The Art of Contentious Encounters*. Berkeley: University of California Press, 1994.